RELIGION
and the
AMERICAN
REVOLUTION

RELIGION
and the
AMERICAN
REVOLUTION

edited by
JERALD C. BRAUER

with contributions by
JERALD C. BRAUER
SIDNEY E. MEAD
ROBERT N. BELLAH

FORTRESS PRESS   Philadelphia

"Christendom, Enlightenment, and the Revolution" by Sidney E. Mead was originally presented, in slightly different form, as one of the Jefferson Memorial Lectures at the University of California, Berkeley, California. "The Revolution and the Civil Religion" by Robert N. Bellah originally appeared, in a shorter version, in *Religious Education* 71, no. 2 (May/June 1976).

Library of Congress Catalog Card Number: 76–9718
ISBN: 0–8006–1241–8

5777D76   Printed in U.S.A.   1-1241

209.73
B

CONTENTS

PREFACE

Almost every conceivable facet and dimension of early American life has been analyzed, studied, celebrated, and praised in recent years. Attention has been paid to the art, music, literature, furniture, and fine arts as well as the cultural and social mores of the Revolutionary epoch. A serious effort has been made to reappraise both the causes and the nature of the American Revolution and the consequent development of the American Constitution. Revisionists have long been at work in an attempt to view the Revolutionary events from other than the traditional perspectives. This is a salutary exercise. Fundamental questions must be asked anew by each generation as it seeks to appropriate and to understand its past. History is constantly in the process of being rewritten.

Religion in the Revolutionary epoch of American life has also received its share of current attention. No longer is it fashionable or possible to assume that there was a direct carry-over from the religious beliefs and practices in the colonies to the growth of the Revolutionary spirit and the carrying through of the Revolution itself. Books and articles are still written about the major contributions of particular religious figures such as Jonathan Mayhew, the great Boston Puritan preacher, or the overall contributions of each of the particular denominations from the Baptists to the Roman Catholics. The exercise of praise, however, hardly contributes to a profounder understanding of the causes and nature of the American Revolution. Religion is one of those forces in American life which people assume was creatively related to the founding days of the Republic. Americans have always held an unusually high degree of respect for religion and its role in their culture. Frequently they have overassessed its creative contributions. In the recent studies, however, a more balanced and hence truer picture of the relationship of religion to the American Revolution has emerged.

When three professors are asked to lecture on three different dimensions of the same subject, one is never certain what might emerge. The most careful planning could go astray. With a subject as vast as the American Revolution, totally diverse essays could be produced by different authors treating the same theme. If the diversity proved to be complementary, or if together the essays conveyed a fuller picture of the same reality, they would represent a degree of cohesiveness. On the other hand, the diversity might result in three totally unrelated, independent, and disconnected essays; in such a case, the three ought not to be put together in a single volume.

Though the three essays prepared for the Armstrong Lectures in religion at Kalamazoo College, Kalamazoo, Michigan dealt with different aspects or dimensions of the relation of religion to the American Revolution, those dimensions were carefully chosen so that whatever diversity of approach prevailed there would nevertheless be a certain degree of cohesiveness. It is interesting to note how many things are held in common by the three essayists.

The three authors, each from his own perspective, assume that there was a close interrelationship between religion and the American Revolution. Each of the three also assumes that this relationship was complex, not simple. Indeed, complexity might be called the key to all three essays: it is in the nature of that complexity that each of the authors grounds the relationship between religion and the American Revolution. Furthermore, all three agree that the Revolution first occurs in the attitudes, mind, or spirit of the American people prior to its outbreak in actual rebellion and warfare; two explicitly quote John Adams's oft-quoted thoughts on that problem. All three rehearse certain of the basic religious concepts such as covenant, consent, fundamental law, and liberty as these related to the emergence and the carrying through of the Revolution. Thus, there is an underlying unity that ties together the three essays even though each deals in its own way with a particular aspect of the problem.

The first essay on "Puritanism, Revivalism, and the American Revolution" seeks to demonstrate the way in which religion helped to produce the Revolutionary spirit and attitude on the part of the American colonists. New England Puritan society was built upon and grew out of a center composed of certain basic religious symbols, beliefs, and attitudes. From the very beginning this center had within it and playing over against it certain other peripheral symbols and beliefs. As New England history unfolded, the central religious symbols brought the peripheral attitudes under attack until they were no longer regarded as tolerable within New England society. This was a basic factor that helped to bring about the revolution in the New England attitude toward England. Furthermore, the Great Awakening functioned in such a way that it not only brought the peripheral symbols of Crown and Parliament under attack but also objected to the very center of Puritan symbols and values with considerable dissatisfaction and discontent. This also led to the creation of a new revolutionary ideology. Hence the first essay argues for a creative relationship between religion and the American Revolution and views that interrelationship as something both subtle and complex.

The second essay on "Christendom, Enlightenment, and Revolution" rejects the over-simple idea that the Puritans alone or primarily were responsible for the coming of the

American Revolution and for the shaping of the Revolutionary epoch in American culture. It was not the religion of American denominations which basically set and legitimated the norms for the American Revolution; rather it was the symbols, concepts, and beliefs of the Enlightenment which provided the legitimation both for the basic Revolutionary ideas and particularly for those ideas which underlay the American Constitution and subsequent American history. Professor Mead is one of a number of distinguished historians who see the Enlightenment not simply as a philosophical movement but primarily as a religious movement. In his judgment it is the Enlightenment as a religious movement which underlies the basic symbols, beliefs, and attitudes of the American Republic, and it is this form of religion that was central to the Revolution and to the shaping of the American nation. Denominational religion, including Puritanism and Revivalism, never clearly understood the implications of the Enlightenment for the founding or the future of the American nation. Thus, the relationship between religion and the American Revolution is located not where historians normally have placed it but at another point.

The third essay on "The Revolution and the Civil Religion" shares the belief that religion and the American Revolution were intimately related; however, it disagrees somewhat with the second essay in arguing that from the very beginning of the American Revolution and the constitutional period of American history there were two great structures of interpretation which underlay both the American Revolution and civil religion. For Professor Bellah, the two are, in a sense, identical. They emerged out of the Christian denominational-biblical tradition on the one hand and Enlightenment utilitarianism on the other hand. These two basic motifs have been intermingled from the very beginning. Thus the relation between religion and the American Revolution was complex and dependent upon several traditions. The essay traces out a movement from the Declaration of Independence with its primary emphasis on virtue and subsidiary concern for self-interest to the Constitution with its basic concern for self-interest. In this chapter, one has a fuller and more subtle exposition of the relationship between religion, civil religion, and the American Revolution.

Taken together, the three essays represent a coordinated and unified effort to gain a new perspective on the way that religion and the American Revolution were interrelated. The relationship is to be seen as complex, yet clear. From this point of view one can proceed to review the wide variety of ways in which religion and American culture have been constantly interrelated throughout American history.

JERALD C. BRAUER

RELIGION
and the
AMERICAN
REVOLUTION

JERALD C. BRAUER

PURITANISM, REVIVALISM, AND THE REVOLUTION

For many years scholars have debated the relationship between religion and revolution. Almost all of the views expressed in the discussions of that basic problem are reflected also in the writings on the relationship between religion and the American Revolution. Earliest interpreters of that intricate relationship could be classified as exemplars of filial piety. They believed that the roots of the American Revolution were to be found primarily within the Puritanism brought from England to American shores. The Puritan world-view as represented by its doughty expositors, the New England clergy, provided the intellectual vision or framework in terms of which the Revolution later was mounted.

That view encountered a number of basic objections. How could it account for the transformation of a theocratic state into a democratic state? Could one demonstrate that the basic ideas espoused by the clergy made any impact on masses of people? At best it might be argued that certain of these basic ideas were taken over by later propagandists and used for their own purposes.

Perhaps the most telling critique of the earliest assumed relationship between Puritanism and the American Revolution is that it stressed certain abstract ideas, theological and philosophical, and so overlooked the real forces that produced the American Revolution. It tended to ignore deep-rooted social tensions that marked mid and later

1

eighteeneth-century American society. It subsumed all
colonial sectional concerns under a basically New England
concern. It failed to see the late eighteenth-century struggle
with England in terms of a long ongoing struggle between
the colonies and the mother country. It paid scant attention
to the economic tensions which slowly developed between
England and the colonies and reached their peak after the
conclusion of the French and Indian War.

The late Hannah Arendt wrote, "The rebellious spirit,
which seems so manifest in certain strictly religious movements in the modern age, always ended in some Great
Awakening or revivalism which, no matter how much it
might 'revive' those who were seized by it, remained politically without consequences and historically futile."[1] Such
a view hardly does justice to the complex realities of the
historical situation which saw the development of the American Revolution. Religion was indeed one of the primary
forces which impelled colonial American people towards
revolution and sustained them in their actions.

In an attempt to prove a connection between religion and
the American Revolution, some historians thought it sufficient to quote sermons that contained words and ideas
similar or identical to political rhetoric of the Revolution.
John W. Thornton is a good example. In the preface to his
The Pulpit of the American Revolution, which appeared in
Boston in 1860, Thornton begins with this statement:

> The true alliance between Politics and Religion is the lesson
> inculcated in this volume of Sermons, and apparent in its
> title. . . . It is the voice of the Fathers of the Republic,
> enforced by their example. They invoked God in their civil
> assemblies, called upon their chosen teachers of religion for
> counsel from the Bible, and recognized its precepts as the
> law of their public conduct. The Fathers did not divorce
> politics and religion, but they denounced the separation as

1. Hannah Arendt, *On Revolution* (New York: Viking Press, 1965), p. 19.

ungodly. They prepared for the struggle and went into battle, not as soldiers of fortune, but, like Cromwell and the soldiers of the Commonwealth, with the Word of God in their hearts, and trusting in him. This was the secret of that moral energy which sustained the Republic in its material weakness against superior numbers, and discipline, and all the power of England. To these Sermons—the responses from the Pulpit—the State affixed its *imprimatur*, and thus they were handed down to future generations with a two-fold claim to respect.[2]

Thornton goes on to say, "In the sermon of 1750 Jonathan Mayhew declared the Christian principles of government in the faith of which Washington, ordained by God, won liberty for America, not less for England, and ultimately for the world.[3] And quite self-consciously, Thornton tied in the American Revolution with the earlier English Puritan Revolution when he stated, "The name of Hugh Peter reminds us that New England shared in English Revolution of 1640; sent preachers and soldiers, aid and comfort to Cromwell; gave an asylum to the tyrannicides, Whalley, Goffe, and Dixwell; reaffirmed the same maxims of liberty in the Revolution of 1688, and stood right on the record for the third revolution of 1776."[4]

Thornton not only sees an intimate connection between religion and the American Revolution; he confines that relationship to Puritanism. Such a view overlooked entirely the Episcopalian contributions made through Virginia leaders. Where the latter have been credited it is usually pointed out that they were no longer genuinely religious but at the very best latitudinarian in their outlook. But even if latitudinarianism is to be understood as a religious movement, one recent historian argued that "the contribution of religious

2. John Wingate Thornton, *The Pulpit of the American Revolution, or the Political Sermons of the Period of 1776* (Boston: Gould and Lincoln, 1860), p. iii.
3. Ibid., p. v.
4. Ibid., p. xx.

latitudinarianism . . . is normally overrated in American history."[5]

If latitudinarianism and Enlightenment are to be understood, in part, as religious movements, as a number of contemporary historians now argue, then the relationship between religion and the American Revolution requires reevaluation. That process is now underway.[6] This paper assumes that fundamental contributions were made by religious movements other than Puritanism and Revivalism, but in this brief essay it is impossible to touch that larger question.

The Thornton preface is a classic example of begging the question of the interrelationship between religion and the American Revolution. Did these abstract, formal theological doctrines relate directly to the political process of the day, or were they primarily rationalizations of fundamental realities which were in no sense theological? Historians of religious thought and institutions in America have paid insufficient attention to these two basic criticisms. They persist in the assumption that formal discourse related directly to the political action of the American Revoltuion.

The problem is to determine, if possible, how New England culture moved through its religious symbols and beliefs from what appeared to be a conserative theocracy to wholehearted support of a revolution. In his stimulating essay "Center and Periphery" Edward Shils provides a perspective which enables one to note how Puritanism's and Revivalism's theological beliefs and symbols helped to create

5. James Hastings Nichols, *Democracy and the Churches* (Philadelphia: Westminister Press, 1951), p. 40.

6. Sidney E. Mead is one of the clearest expositors of the Enlightenment as a religious movement and its consequences for religion and politics in America. Note chapter two in this book, and also his *The Nation With the Soul of a Church* (New York: Harper and Row, 1975). See also Lester D. Joyce, *Church and Clergy in the American Revolution: A Study in Group Behaviour* (New York: Exposition Press, 1966).

a revolution in the colonists' hearts and minds prior to the outbreak of the rebellion.[7]

New England society was founded on and lived out of a clear center, which from its inception contained certain paradoxical or peripheral elements. It is not difficult to locate the realm of values, beliefs, and symbols which gave coherence and meaning to that society. These beliefs and symbols the New Englanders grounded in sacrality or in God himself; they were ultimate, dependent upon the will of God as revealed in Scripture and reconfirmed in nature. Though all of society participated in them and upheld them, they were especially embodied in and manifested by a ruling elite composed of magistrates and ministers. Out of these symbols and beliefs order prevailed both for society at large and for the various subsystems and institutions within it.

Society was a coherent, well-articulated system that exhibited a basic center and contained several peripheral or paradoxical elements. As the historical process unfolded and New Englanders participated in the vicissitudes of historical experience, the center, composed of the symbols, values, and beliefs which initially undergirded order and authority in the colony, became a dynamic ingredient in rebellion against Crown and Parliament.

It is unnecessary and impossible to sketch out the entire process whereby Puritanism and Revivalism, drawing on symbols and beliefs which were central to New England society, helped to overthrow both King and Parliament. An effort will be made to lift up several of these central values and beliefs and to indicate briefly how each underwent a process of transformation and reaffirmation which enabled it to play a direct role in the political processes of the late

7. *Selected Essays by Edward Shils* (Chicago: Center for Social Organization Studies, Department of Sociology, University of Chicago, 1970), pp. 1–14. Taken from Edward Shils, *The Logic of Personal Knowledge* (London: Routledge and Kegan Paul, 1961).

eighteenth century. Fortunately, all of these beliefs and symbols have been carefully analyzed and studied by numerous scholars, and it is unnecessary to spend time on their subtleties and various interconnections.

I

The Puritans who first settled Massachusetts Bay Colony believed that their holy experiment was founded on divine will. They believed that every aspect of their life, both personal and social, was grounded in sacrality. The very fact of their presence in the New World was posited on the assumption that God, in his providence, had saved the discovery of the New World until after the reformation of his church. The Puritans were called by Providence to settle the New World and to establish a "due forme of Government both civill and ecclesiasticall,"[8] grounded on the revealed word of God as encountered in the Scriptures of the Old and New Testaments. Modern society might wish to deny the ultimacy of those beliefs and symbols which undergirded it, but in New England the Puritan concern was the opposite. It heartily affirmed that society existed only in and through divine Providence.

Though predestination was an essential doctrine for the vast majority of Puritans and had consequences both for personal and social life, it cannot in itself be counted as one of the central symbols or beliefs that marked Puritan society. Seven or eight basic symbols, beliefs, or values were closely articulated to form the center as well as the peripheral structure of Puritan society. These were reflected throughout New England economic, political, and family life and class structure, as well as in the institutions of the churches and schools. They were held tenaciously and incarnated by the

---

8. John Winthrop, "Christian Charity" in Perry Miller and Thomas Johnson, eds., *The Puritans: A Source Book of Their Writings* (New York: Harper Torchbooks, 1963), 1:197.

ruling elite in each of the subsystems and institutions. They initially provided resources for order and stability, but later they served to create dissatisfaction and revolution.

One of the most important symbols and values in the entire Puritan cultural system is covenant. This symbol was one of the most basic and pervasive in Puritan society, and it touched on every aspect of life. Covenant did not represent a means whereby a capricious or even irrational deity gave structure and rationality to his otherwise arbitrary will.[9] Covenant was grounded in Scripture as demonstrated by the way God initially called Israel into being through a covenant with Abraham. To be sure, in his eternal wisdom, God elected those whom he chose for eternal life and banned the remainder to perdition, but the way he chose to make known his election was through his Word and Spirit, which created a relationship of covenant between himself and each of his elect; thus, the relation between God and the individual was grounded on covenant.

Three things are essential for the Puritan understanding of covenant. First, it is absolutely clear that all initiative in the creation and sustenance of covenant is in God's hands. He creates, initiates, and sustains the covenant relationship. It is purely an act of grace on God's side. On the other hand, the covenant is, in the second place, conditional. That is, God lays down the basis of covenant and the terms of its fulfillment, and if man fails to fulfill it, the covenant is broken. Judgment and punishment ensue. A third thing to note about the covenant is its communal nature. Though it is grounded in the relationship between God and the

9. There is a basic disagreement on this point. Perry Miller argued that a covenant represented Puritan attempts to soften the irrational and arbitrary act of double predestination; see his "The Marrow of Puritan Divinity," *Errand into the Wilderness* (New York: Harper Torchbooks, 1956), pp. 65, 69. Leonard J. Trinterud established the fact that covenant theology was operative before Calvin's *Institutes* and that it was present in English divinity as early as William Tyndale, whom many regard as the first English Puritan; see Trinterud's "The Origins of Puritanism," *Church History* 20 (1951): 37–57.

individual, its purpose is not simply the salvation of individuals but rather the creation of a people. Individuals are not covenanted to God singly, in a lonely relationship. Though the relationship between God and the soul is highly individual and subjective, it occurs only in the context of a community, the church. Churches are collections of individuals covenanted with each other to form a congregation of fellow believers. There is no true manifestation of the church apart from fellow believers owning a covenant with God and with each other.

The basic symbol or belief in the covenant as the way in which God, man, and fellow believers are related carried over into every aspect of Puritan life. Just as the relation between God and man, and between man and fellow men in the church, was grounded on covenant so was the body politic. Before the Pilgrims landed they formulated the Mayflower Compact based upon the concept of the church covenant. In his famous sermon on "Christian Charity," John Winthrop reminded the Puritans that they had covenanted together to undertake a common task; the entire Massachusetts Bay effort was interpreted as a covenant between those engaged in a common enterprise and as a covenant between all the people and God.[10] This symbol is found in diaries, in letters, in countless sermons preached in the context of regular services, and in sermons on great occasions stretching from Winthrop's "Christian Charity" through fast-day and election-day sermons up to and through the very Revolution itself. The commercial charter which the Puritans turned into a political constitution for their holy commonwealth was looked upon as a special act of Providence sealing the covenant made with his people.[11]

A second fundamental belief and central value of Puritan society was the symbol of consent. This too was grounded

10. John Winthrop, "Christian Charity," p. 198.
11. Charles M. Andrews, *The Colonial Period of American History* (New Haven: Yale University Press, 1934), I:431–461.

in Puritan religious experience and tested in day-to-day historical experience. Puritan society was inconceivable apart from the reality of consent. Though God predetermined who was to be saved, it was also his will that election would be made manifest to believers through their conversion. Without a profound, existential religious experience of conversion one could not be a Christian. This was the religious basis of Puritan dissatisfaction with the Reformation in the Church of England: the church was made up primarily of lukewarm Christians who had never experienced the shattering judgment and spiritual rebuilding of the conversion experience.

Conversion represented human consent to the reality of divine election. It was God's will that man consent to the reality of his sinfulness and in the experience of that degradation consent to the reality of divine forgiveness in Jesus Christ. Only in that way would the covenant be owned. God did not strike the elect with a thunderbolt or magically transform a person from sinner to saint. The process of election was internalized through key experiences in life which culminated in human acceptance of salvation. It involved a self-conscious decision to consent to God's will for forgiveness.

The theme of consent runs throughout Puritan society. Just as man consents to God's judgments and divine activities, so the consent of man is required at all key points in human existence. When one joined a congregation one had to demonstrate the truth and validity of one's consent to divine will, and upon acceptance by the congregation one had to consent to join that congregation and to abide by its rules. Therefore, no church had the power to force its will upon any other church. Each congregation was a full and complete church in and of itself, and through consent of its members could make all decisions concerning its own welfare.

Above all, a minister could not be imposed on a congregation by any power from the outside, even by the magistrate. Members of the congregation consented to their own minister. Also in the body politic, consent was required at all key points. Magistrates, deputies, and selectmen had to go through a process of nomination and election by freemen. Without consent they could not rule. Even the militia chose their own officers. Thus the symbol of consent was deeply imbedded in the very matrix of values out of which New England society lived. It cannot be denied that consent operated in New England society in such a way that a relatively small group of elite magistrates and deputies managed to retain control of the colony. But that is not the point. They retained their role as a special elite in society only insofar as they embodied the main values of the people and made necessary adjustments in order to retain consent.

The rule of fundamental law and its absolute necessity was another central belief or value of the Massachusetts Bay Colony.[12] Law was not simply a necessity because of the fallen nature of mankind and the consequent war of all against all. It was more than simply a deterrent against anarchy and chaos. Law was, beyond that, a positive reality which provided structure and order for life so that humanity could realize its full potential in mutual service as well as the fulfillment of its responsibilities to God. Law provided the framework within which a people could live out their covenant responsibilities to God and to each other. It offered not only guidelines but a lure toward the good life.

Law was a structure in which and under which all people lived and worked. No person and no group was above the law and each found their mutual responsibilities properly defined in it. At its best law represented God's own will for the cosmos. In its historic reality, it evidenced the

12. Alice M. Baldwin, *The New England Clergy and the American Revolution* (Durham, North Carolina: Duke University Press, 1928), pp. 12–21.

particular way the English people had worked out their destiny under God's law. Law required both power and authority, but it also provided the limits in terms of which power and authority could and ought to be exercised.[13] It was effectual only because it participated in and was transcended by sacrality. God was both its source and its end so that no person or group, however representative or symbolic of the law, stood beyond it. Though fundamental law provided an essentially conserving force for Puritanism, it became, under other circumstances, a source of protest against both Crown and Parliament.

A fourth central value for Puritan society was a profound belief in an organic society ordained by God. Whatever democratic elements early New England society possessed, it certainly lacked any view of egalitarianism. Society was built on a clear, ordered structure. As in the medieval view of the body politic, society was built solidly on a hierarchical arrangement. It was not as complex or well ordered as the English society from which it derived. Perhaps one could call it a simplification of and variation on the English class-system which had a hereditary monarchy on top, followed in descending succession by clearly demarked classifications of nobility, a complex church hierarchy, a landed gentry, a rising merchant class, simple yoemen, and vast numbers of unfranchised people who fitted none of those categories.

It has been said that the clearly ordered society of New England consisted of basically two classes and that the lines between these two were constantly shifting. One class was composed of people of quality or the rich and the other involved common folk or the not-so-rich, though financial status was not the only distinguishing mark between the

13. John Barnard, *The Throne Established by Righteousness* (Boston, 1734) in A. W. Plumstead, *The Wall and the Garden: Selected Massachusetts Election Sermons 1670–1755* (Minneapolis: University of Minnesota Press, 1968, pp. 252–67. Ebenezer Pemberton, *The Divine Origin and Dignity of Government Asserted* (Boston, 1710), pp. 10, 17–18, 96–98. Baldwin, *New England Clergy*, pp. 32–46.

two groups. In addition to money and particularly land, the heritage and background one brought from England was important, as was one's status in the church and in the various civic functions within the community.[14]

In New England the first group consisted of a small number of people such as the magistrates and other political officers, the ministers, the merchants, and the slowly increasing number of professional people such as doctors, lawyers, and teachers. The second group was composed largely of small landowners whose material resources were not yet sufficient to establish them as members of the first class.

Puritan sermons and tracts abound with references to the good ruler.[15] In fact, Winthrop was typical of a ruler who reminded both himself and his fellow magistrates of the nature and extent of their responsibilities. The point is that New England society believed that a small number of people symbolized the deepest values and beliefs of their system as long as that elite remained faithful embodiments of those beliefs.

The essentially conservative New England Puritan belief in the hierarchically ordered society had both within its theory and in its practice forces which, under the proper historical circumstances, could become highly critical if not revolutionary. The Achilles' heel of the New England Puritan value system and belief pattern was in their loyalty to Crown and Parliament. Englishmen were bred to respect and honor the Crown even when they disagreed with it. The founders of New England were Englishmen. They represented several generations of frustrated efforts at religious reform, and they sought out a new habitation because they were convinced that their lives and fortunes were in

14. Robert E. Brown, *Middle-Class Democracy and the Revolution, 1691–1780* (New York: Harper Torchbooks, 1969), pp. 38–119. Stephen Foster, *Their Solitary Way* (New Haven: Yale University Press, 1971), pp. 33–40.
15. Foster, *Their Solitary Way*, pp. 67–98, See also Samuel Willard, *The Character of a Good Ruler* . . . (Boston, 1694); Benjamin Wadsworth, *Rulers Feeding and Guiding This People* . . . (Boston, 1716).

danger at the hands of the Crown. They were not free to worship God as they ought or to shape their lives accordingly.

Nevertheless, the New England Puritans did not break with the central English symbol of the role and power of the English Crown. They appealed from a misguided and misinformed Crown to the Crown as it ought to be in its purity. Frustrated in their attempts to achieve religious reform through the necessary political means, Puritans in England early turned to an alliance with Parliament and looked to it more and more as the central symbol of order, justice, and power in English society. Those Puritans who came to New England shared that tradition.

New England Puritans always felt uneasy with the Stuarts, but they remained ambiguously faithful to belief in the Crown. They insisted on the validity of their charter because it was granted by the Crown, but they resisted every effort on the part of the Crown to interpret it, modify it, or take it back. The Puritans were not opposed to the Crown; rather they held an ideal of it which was totally at variance with its actuality in English history. Their view of the Crown was what Shils defined as peripheral to the center of seventeenth-century English ideals and beliefs. But not only was their view of the Crown peripheral; their geographical location itself made the Crown peripheral to their everyday experience. Though there were ample symbols of the Crown in the flag and other officials, the symbol itself was well over three thousand miles distant and lacked means of actualizing its presence. Early in New England experience Endicott got in trouble with his fellow New Englanders when he cut the cross out of the British flag and so symbolized Puritan discontent at the Crown obstinately misinformed concerning the Christian religion. In fear of losing their charter, fellow Puritans made every effort to cover this blunder.

Central to the matrix of New England Puritan values and

beliefs was the symbol of Parliament as the guardian and repository of English liberties and responsibilities. Uneasy with a Crown that refused to understand itself or the Christian religion in a proper light, New England Puritans quickly aligned themselves with the Parliamentary cause during the English Puritan Revolution. They paid the price with the loss of their charter at the time of the Restoration. Further, they had to reaffirm their loyalty to the Crown though they did their best to maintain as many as possible of the privileges and prerogatives which they had so carefully built up over forty-odd years. New England had to bow to the inevitable and accept a royal governor and a large number of his underlings in various key posts. In the New England body politic the Puritans had not strayed so far from the symbol of the Crown that they were utterly unable to live with it in their system of values. They reaffirmed their earlier belief in the value and significance of the Crown and hoped for better days.

The Puritans were fully aware of the exclusion controversy waged in England at the time of the Glorious Revolution. They were delighted at the accession of William and Mary to the throne, and they applauded the emergent supremacy of Parliament. The preeminence of Parliament in conjunction with a clearly limited Crown emerged as central symbols in English life, and these were shared by New England as well. However, there was a difference in the function of Parliament and Crown in the central value system of New England society.

Although the Puritans were content to live as part of the British empire and gave genuine obeisance both to Parliament and Crown, there remained an ambiguity and a paradoxical relation between these two central symbols of English society and their function in the center of New England society. New Englanders constantly harked back to their original charter as well as their rights and liberties not only as Engishmen but as New Englanders in the New

World. Election-day sermons are demonstrable proof of this attitude.[16] Under the impact of historic events New England was led to the point where Parliament and Crown in the New England value system clashed with the English vision of the function and role of Crown and Parliament both within England and within the British empire.

As a result of the economic problems caused by the French and Indian War, economic problems and readjustments within England itself and throughout the empire, basic changes in the structure of Parliament, the stepped-up campaign for bishops by the Episcopal church in the colonies, and the continuing geographical distance between the colonies and the homeland, there developed a growing sense of dissatisfaction and distrust on the part of the American colonies and New England in particular.[17]

In the face of growing differences with England, the response of New England was comparable to their earlier response at the time of Charles I. They held a utopian view of the Crown and Parliament. Puritans appreciated and looked to the Hanoverian family for understanding and support, just as they respected and honored the function and role of Parliament. They blamed the growing difficulties on stupid and conniving politicians who were not genuinely concerned with the true interests of England, Crown, Parliament, or New England. The initial opposition to the Grenville government drew upon the whole arsenal of the central values and beliefs of Puritan society, including Crown and Parliament. Consent, covenant, the structure of fundamental law, the stability of their ordered society, Crown and Parliament, and their belief in liberty were all employed in arguments by clergymen and politicians alike.[18] What started as an uncomfortable disagreement between colony

---

16. Thornton, *The Pulpit of the American Revolution*, passim; Plumstead, *The Wall and the Garden*, passim.
17. Brown, *Middle-Class Democracy*.
18. Baldwin, *New England Clergy*, pp. 105–121.

and British empire escalated into a basic feeling of distrust and fear which eventuated in rebellion on the part of the colonists.

A number of events conspired to threaten the traditional liberties of the Englishman and the well-established hard-won liberties of the New Englanders themselves. As a result of the missionary activity of the Society for the Propagation of the Gospel throughout the colonies and particularly in New England, and with the introduction of the Church of England worship in Boston, the very heart of New England, clergy and laity alike began to fear a vast plot to overthrow the liberties of their churches and to establish the Church of England.

Carl Bridenbaugh sketched out the social and political implications of the struggle over the attempt to establish bishops in the American colonies.[19] The high point of agitation for bishops coincided with the growing alienation between the colonies and England over new taxes and a new system of tax collection, and a mounting debate over the extent and nature of Parliament's authority in relation to the colonies. All segments of colonial society felt they had a stake in the outcome of these disagreements. As Parliament defined its power over the colonies and exercised that power in ways unacceptable to New Englanders, the initial ambiguity over Crown and Parliament in the center of New England values and beliefs grew into outright opposition. Unambiguous powerful symbols and beliefs within the center forced the symbols of Crown and Parliament into an increasingly peripheral position until, in the name of the very center itself, they were eliminated.

Those placed in power as representatives of the Crown

---

19. Carl Bridenbaugh, *Mitre and Sceptre: Transatlantic Faiths, Ideas, Personalities, and Politics* (New York: Oxford University Press, 1962), pp. 171–340. As a result of this definitive study one can see the growth of New England distrust of bishops to a fear of a Crown and Parliament bent on imposing an abominable system to an ideology of opposition.

and Parliament could not understand the agitation, the distrust, and the growing hatred against the established system. A number of them never did understand why the Revolution came about, and so they found themselves loyalists and had to flee when their time came.[20] That which started as an incoherent and fearful discontent slowly crystalized into ever more precise opposition and action.

Puritanism was one of the most effective forces in colonial America in "mobilizing the general mood" and effectively organizing both ideas and actions in opposition to Crown and Parliament.[21] Puritanism had consistently pointed to, preached, and attempted to live out the central values and beliefs that gave coherence and meaning to Puritan society. Although these symbols were not identical in content with those held by the first generation founders of New England, they were clearly derivative from that matrix of beliefs and values. In the hands of the Puritan descendents of the Revolutionary epoch, symbols such as covenant, consent, fundamental law, and liberty were used first to criticize and finally to undercut two other central symbols that had always been held with a certain degree of ambiguity, namely Crown and Parliament. These same beliefs and symbols

20. Bernard Bailyn, "Central Themes of the Revolution" in Stephen G. Kurtz and James H. Hutson, *Essays on the American Revolution* (New York: W. W. Norton, 1973), pp. 15–18.

21. Ibid., p. 11. Bailyn's use of C. Geertz's concept of ideology as one means of explaining the process whereby ideas effect social change represents a major advance in the interpretation of the American Revolution. This is equally applicable to the role of Puritanism and the Great Awakening. "Formal discourse becomes politically powerful when it becomes ideology; when it articulates and fuses into effective formulations opinions and attitudes that are otherwise too scattered and vague to be acted upon; when it mobilizes a general mood, 'a set of disconnected, unrealized private emotions,' into 'a public possession, a social fact'; when it crystallizes otherwise inchoate social and political discontent and thereby shapes what is otherwise instinctive and directs it to attainable goals, when it clarifies, symbolizes, and elevates to structured consciousness the mingled urges that stir within us. But its power is not autonomous. It can only formulate, reshape, and direct forward moods, attitudes, ideas, and aspirations that in some form, however crude or incomplete, already exist." Ibid., p. 11.

articulated by the New England Puritans merged with parallel, similar, and, at time, even dissimilar values and beliefs from other sources to produce a new ideology which formed and shaped the resistance of the American colonies against Crown and Parliament.

II

The emergence of Revivalism in the 1730s marked a new phase in the development of Christianity in American culture, and it both renewed Puritanism and presented it with a fundamental challenge.[22] Though Revivalism grew out of Puritanism, it was equally a child of the continental Pietistic movement that swept Europe and England in the late seventeenth and early eighteenth centuries and made its way to American shores. On the surface Revivalism appears as a form of Puritanism whereas in fact it is just the opposite of Puritanism at many key points. Both movements share the centrality of the conversion experience; however, in Puritanism the conversion experience was set solidly in the middle of a complex social and institutional structure. In one sense, Revivalism as a religious movement excised the concept of conversion out of Puritanism and cast it loose in a highly individualistic and subjectivistic fashion.[23]

Many of the central values and symbols of New England society were brought under attack directly or indirectly by the Great Awakening, the first expression of Revivalism in

22. Two excellent essays that deal with this issue are in James Ward Smith and A. Leland Jamison, *Religion in American Life* (Princeton, N.J.: Princeton University Press, 1961): by Perry Miller, "From Covenant to Revival," 1:322–360, and by H. Richard Niebuhr, "The Protestant Movement and Democracy in the United States," I:26–50.

23. One of the first to note this important shift, though it was not documented thoroughly, was Herbert W. Schneider in a work too often overlooked, *The Puritan Mind* (New York: Henry Holt and Co., 1930), pp. 106–110. This analysis was carried further by the late Joseph Haroutunian in *Piety Versus Moralism: The Passing of New England Theology* (New York: Henry Holt and Co., 1932), pp. xxi ff., 9–12.

American culture.[24] Each of the basic symbols and beliefs that marked the center of New England Puritan culture will be reviewed insofar as they were modified or attacked by the Great Awakening. The consequence of newly emerging symbols and beliefs of Revivalism will be seen as a resource which fed into the growing opposition to Crown and Parliament and helped to mobilize and give structure to widespread unorganized feelings of discontent. Thus Revivalism, along with Puritanism, helped to prepare and sustain an attitude in the American colonies which eventuated in rebellion and revolution.[25]

Among the new beliefs, symbols, and values which marked Revivalism, four in particular stand out as critical and having consequences for the development of new attitudes. Primary among these was Revivalism's belief in and creation of the new man. Conversion of a sinner denoted the death of the old man and the emergence or rebirth of a new man. The converted believer died to sin, to old habits and patterns, and emerged a new man open to new responsibilities and new forms of discipline.

A radical break occured in the life process of the converted person. Before conversion, one was alienated from God and one's fellow human beings, wallowing in misdirected affections or slowly dying in indifference toward the true goals of life, and wholly committed to an unspiritual life. As a result of conversion, a human being was totally turned about. A conversion experience marked an ontological change in which the old Adam died and a new believer in Christ was born. This profound, shattering, all-embracing experience transformed the total life of the believer and

24. Alan Heimart and Perry Miller, eds., *The Great Awakening: Documents Illustrating the Crisis and its Consequences* (New York and Indianapolis: Bobbs Merrill, 1967). The entire introduction is given to this analysis.

25. In the following section no attempt will be made to document from sources the four salient points from the Great Awakening as even a quick reading selected from the works of J. Edwards, G. Whitefield, G. Tennet, or any of the major figures of the Revival will exhibit these factors.

had far-reaching consequences for his entire existence.

Both Puritan and Anglican divines immediately saw the consequences of this startling emphasis on the new man. Leading Boston clergy who attacked the gradual encroachment of the British on New England rights also attacked what they felt were the destructive tendencies of the Great Awakening not only in Jonathan Edwards but especially in his less sophisticated and less intelligent cohorts.[26] Puritanism was built upon the centrality of the doctrine of conversion, and in New England it was held that only truly converted people could be accepted into full church membership. By 1636 the holy commonwealth was ruled only by those who had demonstrated a full conversion experience to the satisfaction of the saints.

Once New England settled for the Half-Way covenant, the centrality and necessity of conversion receded into the background. It was not that New England Puritanism gave up on conversion; on the contrary, the ministers constantly hoped for, prayed for, and worked for periods of "refreshing" as they called it. There were a number of such periods in New England church life; however, they were never widespread nor did they exhibit a high degree of intensity.[27] The Puritan doctrine of conversion was never divorced from the doctrine of the covenant or the holy community. The emotional drive of conversion was always carefully balanced by the function and role of reason and seen in the context of a biblical hermeneutic. Hence, it was not the doctrine of the new man which was predominant in the New England Puritan concept of conversion but rather the doctrine of the converted man as a recruit for both congregation and com-

26. Joseph Tracy, *The Great Awakening: A History of the Revival of Religion in the Time of Edwards and Whitefield* (Boston: Tappen and Dennet, 1842), pp. 302–387. See also Edwin Gaustad, *The Great Awakening* (New York: Harper and Row, 1964), pp. 80–101.

27. Jonathan Edwards, *The Works of Jonathan Edwards*, ed. C. C. Goen (New Haven: Yale University Press, 1972), vol. 4, *The Great Awakening*, pp. 4–5, 114–115, 145–146, 562.

munity. Conversion was the bedrock for total citizenship in all aspects of the holy commonwealth. Conversion embodied a high degree of subjectivity, but it remained in a delicate balance both with the objectivity of total community involvement and the balancing power of reason.

The Great Awakening has been interpreted as the first colony-wide movement that bound together many diverse interests among the thirteen colonies and provided a thread of unity that ran throughout the group. Some historians have gone so far as to argue that it was the first movement that gave the colonies any sense of common identity.[28] Itinerant ministers, exemplified by the indefatigable George Whitfield, traveled from colony to colony bearing their message of repentance and redemption. Whitfield's numerous trips to America and his crisscrossing the colonies and appearing in every major city documents the extent and importance of the movement. The significance of the Great Awakening lies not only in its pervasiveness throughout the colonies but equally, if not more, in those ideas and beliefs which it injected into mid-eighteeneth-century American culture.

Rebirth led to a new man, a new being. Though the new man was not totally discontinuous from the old man, emphasis was on the new. A heightened sense of decision led to a high degree of self-consciousness concerning one's difference from all those who surrounded him in society. The converted believer basked in his own uniqueness, which inevitably led to an intense dissatisfaction with the traditional, with things as they were.

Though the converts of the Great Awakening were committed to the same central grouping of values and symbols as were the Puritans, they tended to hold these with a degree of absoluteness which made them highly critical of the elite in society who symbolized those values but did not

28. William W. Sweet, *Revivalism in America* (New York: Charles Scribner's Sons, 1944), pp. 24–27.

live them fully and completely. The new man was to be new and to express his commitments fully and completely. The converted believer saw no shades of gray but only extremes of good and bad, right and wrong; there was nothing in between. When the new man questioned the traditional values and beliefs it was usually not to overthrow them or to set them aside but to argue for a complete, full, logical application. Often that so-called logical application led to direct opposition to the values themselves.

Not only did the Great Awakening create a belief in the new man which tended to question traditional values; it also created an image of a new age. This was not a repudiation of earlier Puritan ideals; rather it was an attempt to carry them a step further and to apply those values directly to American society at a particular moment in history. In his *History of the Work of Redemption* Jonathan Edwards sketched out a new version of the chosen people theme.[29] No longer were the Puritans only a light and an example to the rest of the world with regard to a "due forme of Government both civill and ecclesiasticall"; now they had moved far beyond that.

In Edwards's view America was to be the center of God's kingdom on earth; it was here that the new age would dawn. The revivals themselves were part of the proof of this concept.[30] God's Spirit had long been at work in history to bring to fruition his plans for the whole cosmos. His kingdom had in a sense already come in part and was now gradually unfolding. Prior to the final judgment and overthrow of all evil, human history would first go through a time of tribulation and then would enter a period of great creativity and goodness. Edwards was convinced that history had reached that point and the Spirit of God was about

29. *The Works of President Edwards in Four Volumes* (New York: Leavitt and Allen, 1857) I:491–497.
30. Edwards, *The Works of Jonathan Edwards*, "Some Thoughts Concerning the Revival," p. 353.

to pour itself forth throughout the world in a new, fresh, and creative way. America was to be the center of that movement, and it was from this point in the world that God's Spirit would go forth to all mankind. Edwards's vision of a total world history culminated in a new age of the Spirit centered in America, and in New England in particular.[31]

The combined vision of the new man and the new age appeared in a context conducive to building a sense of uniqueness and individuality among the American colonies. New men participating in the first stages of a new age could easily become disenchanted with the more restrictive traditions of an old age. There was a sense in which a number of the leaders and new converts in Revivalism had their sights fixed backwards upon a glorious past that was to be reconstituted, but it was equally true that even those older values were now seen by many in the context of a new age and a new epoch. Traditional authority, whether local magistrates, Parliament, or Crown, looked quite different from the perspective of a dawning new age. Though it is difficult to document the exact degree of Revivalism's influence in encouraging a new ideology critical of British rule, it is nevertheless interesting to note the number of leaders and laity from the ranks of Revivalism who made common cause with the leaders of the Revolution.

Perhaps even more important than belief in the new man and in the new age was Revivalism's insistence on the centrality of the Holy Spirit and its consequence for the religious life. The doctrine of the Spirit was at the base of both the conversion experience which created the new man and of the new age brought into being through God's providential action. The Spirit was a great equalizer in all religious life. Only those led of the Spirit could exemplify and carry genuine religious authority. Only those reborn of the Spirit could be entrusted with ministry, and those

31. Ibid. p. 358.

who were not so converted were in fact destructive of Christianity.

When employed outside the context of strong traditions, the biblical injunction that "the Spirit bloweth where it listeth" tended to undercut all religious authority and in many cases all forms of authority whatsoever. It was the children of the Great Awakening who first seriously questioned the authority and the power of the traditional ministers as well as the right and authority of the magistrates to lay down the conditions of religious expression through worship.

Professor Richard L. Bushman sketched out the consequences of Revivalism and its emphasis on the Spirit for the social order in Connecticut immediately prior to the Revolution.[32] He quoted Jonathan Todd in *Civil Rulers* to the effect that Revivalists "would put down all rule, and all authority and power among men: pleading in defense of their licentious doctrine that Christ hath made all his people kings." And from Todd he also cited the Revivalists' disrespect for leaders, both clerical and lay, who were not properly converted, how they regarded such "leaders and rulers of this people as unconverted and *opposers* of the work of God, and usurping an authority that did not belong to them."[33] Bushman also pointed out that Samuel Johnson, the great Episcopalian leader in Connecticut, lumped together Revivalism and democracy in their disrespect for proper authority: "The prevalency of rigid enthusiastical conceited notions and practices in religion and republican mobbish principles and practices and policy, being most on

32. Richard L. Bushman, *From Puritan to Yankee: Churches and Social Order in Connecticut, 1690–1765* (New Haven: Yale University Press, 1967).

33. Jonathan Todd, *Civil Rulers the Ministers of God: . . . Election Day Sermon, May 11th, 1749* (New London, 1949), p. 2. Quoted in Bushman, *From Puritan to Yankee*, p. 271.

a level and each thinking himself an able divine and states-
man: hence perpetual feuds and factions in both.[34]

One cannot deny the widespread outbreak of schism,
disagreement, and infighting within the various churches as
a consequence of Revivalism. Ecclesiastical authorities
were fought or ignored. In their anxiety to win full freedom for their own forms of worship without paying any tax
to support religious forms which they did not believe,
Revivalists waged a steady campaign against all forms of
authority, both clerical and lay magistrate, in an effort to
achieve full freedom for themselves. They did not hesitate
to attack clerical leadership which appeared unconverted,
too traditionally oriented, and a danger to the Revivalists'
conception of the Christian faith.

So churches were split into several camps—old side, new
side, old light, new light, moderates, and separatists. The
fact that Revivalists were willing to attack traditional
authority was in itself a demonstration that in the name of a
so-called just cause traditional authority could be directly
attacked. Revivalists did not hesitate to point out what
they claimed to be inconsistency on the part of those Puritan
descendants who fought to retain their liberty against the
encroachment of possible bishops but refused to extend full
liberty to their fellow believers who could no longer worship with them. When a movement has successfully attacked the authority of clergy and magistrates, they are prepared by habit to take on, if necessary, Crown and Parliament.

Revivalism, which emerged in part out of Puritanism,
shared most of the central beliefs and symbols of Puritanism
itself; however, the Great Awakening held and embodied
these same beliefs in such a way that the believers tended to
be highly critical of those same values and beliefs as em-

34. Ibid., p. 273.

bodied in the contemporary elite of the day. They saw the Puritans as unfaithful to their own basic beliefs and unable to carry them through to their logical consequences. Revivalists held what might be called a utopian view of the Puritan values and beliefs. Ultimately they replaced the traditional elite figures of authority, the clergy and traditional lay magistrates, with a new figure, a new man—any man who had been reborn in the Spirit and was living out the converted life. Thus the layman emerged as the central figure in the Christian community, prepared to judge all people and authority in terms of the presence of the Spirit.

III

Revolution does not come easily to an essentially conservative society. Armed opposition to Crown and Parliament came as a surprise even to the colonial opposition leaders. The true Revolution first occurred in the hearts and minds of colonists as they found it increasingly difficult to square their perception of what it meant to be British subjects with what it was to be American. The source of the problem was neither simple nor immediate. The reasons for discontent were multiple and complex, and their origins were in the founding of the colonies, particularly New England.

Religion was one of the premier forces that brought the colonies into being and provided them with a set of symbols, beliefs, and values which undergirded their society. In at least two respects religion fed directly into the Revolution of heart and mind that preceded the rebellion. Puritanism created the center out of which New England society lived. The symbols, values, and beliefs that comprised that center contained two elements that were always to some degree peripheral, Crown and Parliament. As history unfolded, New Englanders gradually brought these peripheral elements under heavy attack from the center itself so that

Crown and Parliament were viewed as detrimental to the central values of covenant, consent, the rule of fundamental law, the structure of New England's organic society, and the liberties of its inhabitants. Thus Puritanism was a major force in engendering a revolution in attitude toward Crown and Parliament.

In a similar fashion, the Revivalism of the Great Awakening transformed certain of the central symbols of Puritanism and introduced new values and beliefs which questioned not only the authority and function of Crown and Parliament but also the traditional role and power of established clergy and magistrate alike. Revivalism swept the thirteen colonies and provided the first common indigenous movement that they shared. Through its belief in the new man and the new age it taught thousands to question the past and to be open to the future. Inherited forms of community and authority were broken and questioned. Under the free movement of the Spirit of God a leveling dimension was introduced into religious life wherein laity received a new status, and a critical resource became available to all truly converted believers. The daily lives of the colonists reflected a growing degree of frustration and dissatisfaction with the British empire. Revivalism provided one of the most powerful forces that helped to focus that discontent and offered a set of symbols and beliefs which were both a source of criticism and a vision of new possibilities. So Revivalism fed into the American Revolution.

SIDNEY E. MEAD

CHRISTENDOM, ENLIGHTENMENT, AND THE REVOLUTION

As I conceive the study of religion in American history, the basic interpretative motif is experience. This means that one tries to account for those peculiarities of a particular institution that give it its distinctive character by noting the experiences of that institution that are unique to it as compared with the commonly shared experiences of the community of which it is a part.

That Christianity has assumed a distinctive shape in the United States seems obvious.[1] The peculiarities that make it distinctive are the result of the necessity in a relatively brief time to accommodate[2] the old Christianity to a strange new environment in which social and geographical space, and social and political revolution were most prominent.

But it was the experience of the religion of Christendom with religious feudalism defended by civil authority that required revolutionary intellectual and institutional adjustments. By pluralism I mean here a multiplicity of organized religious groups in the commonwealth. Each species of the genus Christian achieves distinctive identity and reason for

1. It seems generally accepted that "the Christianity which developed in the United States was unique. It displayed features which marked it as distinct from previous Christianity in any other land." Kenneth Scott Latourette, *A History of the Expansion of Christianity* (New York: Harper & Bros., 1937–45), 4:424.
2. For a definition of "accommodate" as distinct from "adjust" and "adapt" see John Dewey, *A Common Faith* (New Haven: Yale University Press, 1934), pp. 15–17.

independent being by its peculiar emphasis on one or more of the doctrines shared by all. In the strange chorus of the Christian denominations in the United States they all sing the same song but with different tunes.

The internalization of religion in the eighteenth century, with consequent separation of "salvation" from responsibility for the instituted structures of society, enabled Christians to accept pluralism and religious freedom without feeling a necessity to come to terms with it theologically. They were not inclined to look this gift horse in the mouth. Had they done so they might have discovered that it was a Trojan horse in the Christian citadel. Christians should have learned to be wary of gifts bearing Greeks.

In our pluralistic society, if one presumes to talk about "religion" a decent respect for his listeners requires that he try to make clear what *he* has in mind. Religion is a subject formally dealt with in almost every university discipline and, naturally, in each spoken of in the particular dialect of the tribe. Because we recognize concepts by the words they usually come clothed in, specialists often find it difficult to recognize even one of their own favorite concepts when it is disguised in the terminology of another academic ghetto.[3] Therefore the primary purpose of attempting to define "religion" is to ask whether perhaps a consensus in the understanding of what we are talking about is concealed under the many different guises in which the concept appears. It seems to me that such a consensus exists, or is emerging.

3. H. Richard Niebuhr was always acutely aware of the problems pluralism posed for dialogue. For example: "Every effort to deal with the history of ideas is beset by hazards. Semantic traps are strewn along the way of the inquirer; such words as democracy, liberty, justice, etc., point to different concepts or varying complexes of concepts as they are used in different periods of history and by different men. The unuttered and frequently unacknowledged presuppositions of those who employ them also vary; and since meaning largely depends on context the difficulties of understanding what is meant are increased by the difficulty of ascertaining what is at the back of the minds. Our hazards are multiplied when the ideas in question are of a moral and religious sort." "The Idea of Covenant and American Democracy," *Church History* 23 (June 1954): 126.

In 1835 Alexis de Tocqueville, that aboriginal Delphic oracle of things American, noted that no societies have ever managed without general acceptance by the people of some "dogmatic beliefs, that is to say, opinions which men take on trust without discussion." Without such beliefs "no common action would be possible, and . . . there could be no body social." If society is to exist "it is essential that all the minds of the citizens" be "held together by some leading ideas; and that could never happen unless each of them sometimes came to draw his opinions from the same source and was ready to accept some beliefs ready made."[4]

Tocqueville's view has become a commonplace, enabling Robert Bellah in presenting his view of "American Civil Religion" to note:

> It is one of the oldest of sociological generalizations that any coherent and viable society rests on a common set of moral understandings about good and bad, right and wrong, in the realm of individual and social action. It is almost as widely held that these common moral understandings must also in turn rest upon a common set of religious understandings that provide a picture of the universe in terms of which the moral understandings make sense.[5]

James Baldwin, in a 1959 essay entitled "The Discovery of What It Means to be an American," says he went to Paris to live because he thought he "hated America." But in the experience of living in Paris and trying to relate his experience to "that of others, Negroes and whites, writers and

4. Alexis de Tocqueville, *Democracy in America,* eds. J. P. Mayer and Max Lerner; trans. George Lawrence (New York: Harper & Row, 1966), Part II, chap. 2, p. 398. Samuel Butler stated Tocqueville's point succinctly: "So it is with most of us: that which we observe to be taken as a matter of course by those round us, we take as a matter of course ourselves." Samuel Butler, *Erewhon, or Over the Range* (New York: The New American Library of World Literature, 1960), p. 138. The complete *Erewhon* was first published in 1872.

5. Robert N. Bellah, *The Broken Covenant: American Civil Religion in Time of Trial* (New York: Seabury Press, 1975), p. xi.

non-writers, I proved, to my astonishment, to be as American as any Texas G.I. And I found my experience was shared by every American writer I knew in Paris." Generalizing from this experience, Mr. Baldwin concluded: "Every society is really governed by hidden laws, by unspoken but profound assumptions on the part of the people." With this insight, he says, "I was released from the illusion that I hated America" and "I was able to accept my role—as distinguished, I must say, from my 'place'—in the extraordinary drama which is America."[6]

Historian Ralph Henry Gabriel rested his delineation of *The Course of American Democratic Thought* on a concept of shared "social beliefs" that emerged by around 1815, serving Americans "as guides to action, as standards by which to judge the quality of social life, and as goals to inspire humane living." This "cluster of ideas and ideals. . . taken together, made up a national faith which, although unrecognized as such, had the power of a state religion."[7] Gabriel concluded that only by understanding this "faith" or "religion" was it possible to understand the middle period of American history.

Anthropologist Ruth Benedict in her now classic *Patterns of Culture* argued: "What really binds men together" in communities "is their culture—the ideas and the standards they have in common."[8] It is these shared beliefs that give them a sense of belonging together and of being different from the peoples of other cultures. To understand a people we must know what those "ideas and standards" are.

Edward Shils, writing on "intellectuals," indicated that

6. James Baldwin, *Nobody Knows My Name: More Notes of a Native Son* (New York: Dell Publishing Co., 1961), pp. 15–19.

7. Randolph Henry Gabriel, *The Course of American Democratic Thought,* 2d ed. (New York: Ronald Press Co., 1956), p. 26.

8. Ruth Benedict, *Patterns of Culture* (Boston: Houghton Mifflin Co., 1959), p. 16.

he assumed that "actual communities [are] bound together by the acceptance of a common body of standards."[9] To him we shall return in another connection.

Sociologists, as the quotation from Bellah suggests, have been quick to call the shared ideas and standards "religious." To Robin M. Williams, Jr., religion is that " 'system of beliefs' that defines the norms for behavior in the society" and "represents a complex of ultimate value-orientations." It follows that "every functioning society has . . . a common religion . . . a common set of ideas, rituals, and symbols" which supply and/or celebrate "an overarching sense of unity." It follows that "no society can be understood without also understanding its religion."[10] Seen in this context, to concentrate exclusively on describing a people's "way of life" as exhibited in their behavior is to miss the primarily important thing—what holds them together in a community.

Paul Tillich expressed the same view in more abstract jargon, as befits a theologian:

> Religion as ultimate concern is the meaning-giving substance of culture, and culture is the totality of forms in which the basic concern of religion expresses itself. In abbreviations: religion is the substance of culture, culture is the form of religion. Such a consideration definitely prevents the establishment of a dualism of religion and culture.[11]

And, finally, Philip Selznick's one-sentence summary: "A democracy is a normative system in which behavior and

9. Edward Shils, "The Intellectuals and the Powers: Some Perspectives for Comparative Analysis," in Philip Rieff, ed., *On Intellectuals* (Garden City, N.Y.: Doubleday & Co., 1970), p. 41.

10. Robin M. Williams, Jr., *American Society: A Sociological Interpretation* (New York: Knopf, 1952), pp. 304–306.

11. Paul Tillich, *Theology of Culture*, ed. Robert C. Kimball (New York: Oxford University Press Galaxy Book, 1964), p. 42.

belonging are judged on the basis of conformity, or lack of it, with the master ideal" shared by the people.[12]

These examples, I trust, are enough to suggest a consensus that the word "religion" is to point to a constellation of shared beliefs respecting the nature of the universe and man's place in it, from which the standards for conduct are supposedly deduced. In this view, when we speak of the religion of an individual or of a community we mean to point to whatever constellation of ideas and standards does in fact give cosmic significance and hence purpose to his or its way of life.[13]

While some of the ideas and beliefs here referred to may be clearly articulated, more commonly they are of the nature of Tocqueville's "opinions which men take on trust without discussion," that is, assume or presuppose. In philosopher Alfred North Whitehead's words, "Religion has been and is now the major source of those ideals which add to life a sense of purpose that is worthwhile." It follows, he added, that "apart from religion, expressed in ways generally intelligible, populations sink into the apathetic task of daily survival, with minor alleviations."[14] In that case, for example, "national security" becomes the ultimate goal that guides national policies.

12. Philip Selznick, "Natural Law and Sociology," in John Cogley et al., *Natural Law and Modern Society* (Cleveland: World Publishing Co., 1966), pp. 158, 170. See also the "Sociological Definition of Religion" developed by Charles Y. Glock and Rodney Stark, *Religion and Society in Tension* (Chicago: Rand McNally & Co., 1965), chap. 1, pp. 3–17.

13. There is considerable evidence from psychiatry that whether or not individuals will hold and cherish such beliefs is not a matter of choice, for without them they die. See, for example, Viktor E. Frankl, *Man's Search for Meaning: An Introduction to Logotherapy*, originally published as *From Death-Camp to Existentialism* (New York: Washington Square Press, n.d.), Part I, "Experiences in a Concentration Camp," pp. 3–148; Bruno Bettelheim, *The Informed Heart: Autonomy in a Mass Age* (Glencoe, Ill.: The Free Press, 1960), passim, but esp. chap. 4, 5; Robert Jay Lifton, *Revolutionary Immortality: Mao Tse-Tung and the Chinese Cultural Revolution* (New York: Random House Vintage Books, 1968).

14. Alfred North Whitehead, "An Appeal to Sanity," in *Essays in Science and Philosophy* (New York: Philosophical Library, 1948), p. 55.

I wish to emphasize three implications of this consensus definition of "religion": (1) that the religion of a society is whatever system of beliefs actually provides cosmic legitimation for its institutions, and for the activities of its people; (2) that every individual, every community, has his or its religion; and (3) that the central content of the religion is what is assumed or presupposed by most believers, that is, has to do with what to them is obvious. Hence Baldwin's reference to the "hidden laws" that govern society. For nothing is more hidden from most persons than the presuppositions[15] on which their whole structure of thinking rests.[16]

However, at least a few reflective individuals in every society *are* conscious of the fact that they hold some "truths to be self-evident"—persons who realize with Franklin that there are some things they have "never doubted." These are the "intellectuals," and, as Shils says, "There would be intellectuals in society even if there were no intellectuals by disposition."[17] Baldwin concluded that their calling was to make others aware of these hidden laws that determine their thinking and acting.

If we presume to talk about "religion" in our pluralistic society we must realize that the word points to a numerous family in which there are hundreds of genera (the world's

15. I am using the words "presupposed," and "presupposition(s)"—for substance thereof at least—with the meaning and connotations developed by R. G. Collingwood in *An Essay on Metaphysics* (Oxford: Clarendon Press, 1940), pp. 21–48.

16. For this reason one cannot understand believers simply by listening to what they profess. We are all Erewhonians in this respect: "It is a distinguishing peculiarity of the Erewhonians that when they profess themselves to be quite certain about any matter, and avow it as a base on which they are to build a system of practice, they seldom quite believe in it. If they smell a rat about the precincts of a cherished institution, they will always stop their noses to it if they can." So, the inadvertent visitor concluded, "they did not know themselves what they believed; all they did know was that it was a disease not to believe as they did." That is a good description of the sectarian mind. Samuel Butler, *Erewhon,* p. 142.

17. Shils, "The Intellectuals and the Powers," p. 29.

religions) and thousands of species and sub-species (e.g., denominations), each with its own protective institutional shell.[18] In such a society one cannot be overtly and socially religious without choosing to associate with one of the thousand or more vigorously competitive species. Such competition tends to induce the members of each species to claim, implicitly at least, to be the only true representatives of the family. I call this the "Parson Thwackum syndrome," for that cleric in Henry Fielding's *History of Tom Jones* stated that position most lucidly: "When I mention religion, I mean the Christian religion; and not only the Christian religion, but the Protestant religion; and not only the Protestant religion, but the Church of England."[19] Thus to Thwackum, Anglican, Protestant, Christian, and religious were synonymous. The Thwackums among us erase all distinctions between family, genus, species, and sub-species of religion. And the Thwackum perspective is not uncommon even among the very learned and sophisticated professors in the prestige theological schools who confuse their beliefs with *the* "authentic faith." Ruth Benedict, recognizing the syndrome, warned "white culture" against its tendency "always to identify our own local ways of behaving with behaviour, or our own socialized habits with Human Nature," and, she might have added, our species of religion with religion.[20]

Further, a genus or species of religion may be defined and defended from two quite different points of view— from that of the insider and from that of an outsider. To the insider, talk and writing about his species of religion is

18. Cf. Dewey, *A Common Faith*, pp. 9–10: "There is no such thing as religion in the singular. There is only a multitude of religions. 'Religion' is a strictly collective term. . . . The adjective 'religious' denotes nothing in the way of a specifiable entity, either institutional or as a system of beliefs. It does not denote anything to which one can specifically point to this and that historic religion or existing church."
19. The Modern Library edition, p. 84.
20. Benedict, *Patterns of Culture*, p. 7.

analogous to autobiography. To the outsider, talk about a species of religion is analogous to biography, the voice of knowledge about.[21] In sophisticated dress this distinction was invoked by H. Richard Niebuhr in his *The Meaning of Revelation*.[22] His use of the terms "inner" and "outer" history has been widely adopted by those who gain a reputation for profound thought by repeating the terminology of a master.

Down through the centuries of Christendom able theologians nourished the belief that there was an absolute and eternal difference in kind between "natural" unregenerate persons (the outsiders) and regenerate "saints" (the insiders). Jonathan Edwards, certainly one of the best and the brightest, etched the line between them with great clarity, arguing that "natural men" could no more understand the "gracious influences which the saints are subjects of" than the person with no sense of taste whatever could apprehend "the sweet taste of honey . . . by only looking on it, and feeling of it."[23] In this obscurantist citadel of euphoric and absolute assurance generations of Christians have smugly found an impregnable defense of their peculiar species of Christianity.

More surprising to me, in 1962 Professor Arthur S. Link applied this distinction to the writing of "secular" history in the twentieth century. Assuming that the historian "is called to be a mere chronicler of the past," he argued that the non-Christian historian's chronicle is subject to "the

21. For the imagery of "autobiography" and "biography" I am indebted to William A. Clebsch's book, *From Sacred to Profane America: the Role of Religion in American History* (New York: Harper and Row, 1968), p. 4.
22. H. Richard Niebuhr, *The Meaning of Revelation* (New York: Macmillan Co., 1946), pp. 81–90. Implied in Niebuhr's view is a defense of his species of Christian faith by removing it from the critical scrutiny of the "external" community. To that degree he stood in the tradition of Jonathan Edwards.
23. Jonathan Edwards, "Religious Affections," in *The Works of President Edwards in Eight Volumes* (Worcester, Mass.: Isaiah Thomas, 1808), Vol. IV: 134.

tyranny of the ego's insatiable demands for its own understanding and control of history." But God gives Christians
"the ability to be good and faithful historians" through the
gift of the Spirit. Therefore the Christian's history, being
"purged of the ego's distortions and perversions," is the
only truly "objective" chronicle. Mr. Link concluded that
"if the writers of the Biblical record were 'inspired,' that
is, given grace to be true historians, then we, too, can be
'inspired' even as we are justified."[24] The reader of Mr.
Link's writings will hereafter note that the author modestly
intimates that they belong in the canon of inspired pro-
nouncements.

From the standpoint of those of us who live outside the
temples in which such grace-endowed fellows dwell, what
religion is can be only an opinion based on inferences drawn
from observation and analysis of what self-styled religious
people do and say, individually and collectively, and of
their explanation and defense of their saying and doing. For
as John Dewey noted, we cannot observe religion-in-general,
but only genera and species of the family.[25]

This is to say that outsiders, for whom religion is as
religion does, can produce only biographies of the species or
genera of religion. And if Jonathan Edwards was, and if
Arthur S. Link is, right, the communication gulf between
insiders and outsiders is impassable. To the outsider the
insider's autobiographical argument is unconvincing or mean-
ingless because he lives in a different world of reality in
which the insider's claim is an obscurantist refuge for all the
species of privatized religiosity. Ruth Benedict delineated
the contrast between the two perspectives, as only an outsider could do, in her contrast between open and closed
groups:

24. Arthur S. Link, "The Historian's Vocation," in *Theology Today* 19
(April 1962): 75–89.
25. Dewey, *A Common Faith*, p. 10.

The distinction between any closed group and outside peoples becomes in terms of religion that between the true believers and the heathen. Between these two categories for thousands of years there were no common meeting-points. No ideas or institutions that held in the one were valid in the other. Rather all institutions were seen in opposing terms according as they belonged to one or the other of the very often slightly differentiated religions: on the one side it was a question of Divine Truth and the true believer, of revelation and of God; on the other it was a matter of moral error, of fables, of the damned and of devils. There could be no question of equating the attitudes of the opposed groups and hence no question of understanding from objectively studied data the nature of this important human trait, religion.[26]

I have argued that the experience of the old Christianity in the New World resulted in the internalizing of Christianity with the consequent separation in principle of one's "salvation" from a sense of responsibility for the social, economic, and political life of his society. The nature of this separation can also be delineated in contemporary sociological language, and my interest in consensus induces me to try to do so.

Talcott Parsons is, I take it, a respectable representative of the discipline that has sometimes aspired to be crowned the modern queen of the sciences. Parsons distinguishes between "cultural systems" and "social systems," and describes the relation between them. "Social systems," he says, "are organized about the exigencies of interaction among acting units, both individual persons and collective units." In analyzing them we merely describe "what in fact is done" or predict "what will be."[27]

On the other hand, "Cultural systems . . . are organized about the patterning of meaning in symbolic systems

26. Benedict, *Patterns of Culture*, p. 8.
27. Talcott Parsons, "The Intellectual: A Social Role Category," in Philip Rieff, ed., *On Intellectuals*, p. 3.

['meaning systems'].["28] As for the relation between them, "meaning systems are always in some respects and to some degree normative in their significance" for action and interaction in the social system. Or, as I would say, the meaning system provides cosmic legitimation for the social system.

Parsons continues: the function of a meaning system is that it specifies "what in some sense *should* be done and evaluate[s] the actual performance accordingly," that is, because it defines what is normal behavior, and is internalized, it stands in judgment over deviant action. This all seems in keeping with the complex definition of "religion" I spelled out above. To me, functionally Parsons's meaning system *is* the religion of the society.

In applying this definition to an understanding of our America, it is natural to suppose that the religion (meaning-system) that legitimates America's social, political, and economic system is Christianity as given institutionalized form in the many denominations. This I have come to believe is a mistake. My thesis—that the internalization of religion beginning with the eighteenth-century revivals effectively separated assurance of "salvation" from a sense of responsibility for the institutions of the convert's society—means just that.[29] This is to say that the species of religion incarnated in the denominations, with their massive institutional

28. Ibid. John Higham seems to combine features of Parsons' "culture systems" and "social systems" in his concept of "ideologies" which, he says, are "those explicit systems of general beliefs that give large bodies of people a common identity and purpose, a common program of action, and a standard for self-criticism. Being relatively formalized and explicit, ideology contrasts with a wider, older, more ambiguous fund of myth and tradition. It includes doctrines or theories on the one hand and policies or prescriptions on the other. Accordingly, it links social action with fundamental beliefs, collective identity with the course of history. . . . Arising in the course of modernization when an unreflective culture fractures, ideology provides a new basis for solidarity." John Hingham, "Hanging Together: Divergent Unities in American History," *Journal of American History* 61, 1 (June 1974):10.
29. For another form of this thesis, extensively developed, see John Herman Randall, Sr. and Jr., *Religion and the Modern World* (New York: Stokes Co., 1929), chap. II, "The Religious Heritage of the Nineteenth Century," pp. 23–44.

inertia, is not the religion that actually sets and legitimates the norms for our society—that the theology of the denominations does not legitimate the political and legal structure of the commonwealth.[30]

It follows that it is not very profitable to go looking for the real theology of our Republic in the dusty historical attics of the institutionalized piosity of our contemporary society. Certainly it is not profitable to look only there. Recognition of this separation was always implicit, for example, in those educators who, while holding that the public schools inculcated the moral and spiritual values of the democracy, were very careful to divorce those values from all species of the religion institutionalized in the nation's sects.

I assume that the general health and well-being of a commonwealth-society hinges upon a harmony between its meaning and social systems—between its religion and its society—and that the theology inculcated by the society's dominant churches suggests the cosmic significance of the norms that are invoked to control behavior in the social, economic, political, and judicial spheres. This is to say that religion is the mainspring of an integrated society. When the mainspring is broken the society runs down. Or, as Alfred North Whitehead expressed it, "Religion has been and is now the major source of those ideals which add to life a sense of purpose that is worthwhile. Apart from religion, expressed in ways generally intelligible, populations sink into the apathetic task of daily survival, with minor alleviations."[31]

That the mainspring of the old-line denominations in

30. Actually this seems to me to be commonly recognized as, for example, in the assertion made by Robert M. Brown that Christianity is not where the "greatest decisions" are made. *The Ecumenical Revolution: An Interpretation of the Catholic-Protestant Dialogue* (Garden City, N.Y.: Doubleday & Co., 1967), p. 307.

31. Whitehead, "An Appeal to Sanity," pp. 55–56. For a powerful use of the mainspring figure, see Adlai Stevenson, "Our Broken Mainspring," in Gerry G. Brown, ed., *Adlai E. Stevenson: a Short Biography* (New York: Barron's Educational Series, 1965), pp. 201–15.

America is broken seems widely assumed today and even
persuasively documented.[32] A few years ago it was exuber-
antly self-confessed by professors in jet-set theological
schools who joined Friedrich Nietzsche's madman in the
secular city's marketplace (for example, in *Time* magazine)
proclaiming the death of God. More recently representatives of these self-liquidating theologians have intimated,
with more than usual insight, that it is their theology that
is dead, or at least like the sheep of Little Bo-Peep, is lost
and they do not know where to find it.[33]

I am willing to take their word for it. But the loss of
their ideology does not perturb me insofar as the welfare
of the Republic is concerned. For I hold that *their* lost
theology is not and never has been the mainspring of that
Republic—that *the* theology of the Republic is that of
"Enlightenment" in Crane Brinton's sense. And it is not
clear that this mainspring is broken. Indeed Michael Novak
was easily able to develop a persuasive argument that it is
very much intact; that, indeed, "the tradition in which intellectuals ordinarily define themselves [today] is that of
the Enlightenment"; that Enlightenment is "the dominant
religion" in contemporary society.[34] And Martin E. Marty,
defender of an implicit but vaguely defined Protestant orthodoxy against "religion in general," has argued that in

32. For example, in Dean M. Kelley's study, *Why Conservative Churches
are Growing: A Study in Sociology of Religion* (New York: Harper & Row,
1972), passim.
33. "Whatever Happened to Theology," *Christianity and Crisis 35*, 8 (May
12, 1975). In this issue twelve eminent theologians address this question.
Although they differ considerably in explanations of why it happened and
when, all seem to agree that theology has disappeared. Among the most
enlightening reasons given is that by Rosemary Ruether: "I believe that the
demise of such systematic theology is not recent but has been in preparation
since the Enlightenment. The attempt to rebuild systematic dogmatics since
the 19th century has finally fallen through" (p. 109). Gordon K. Kaufman
laments, "The once proud queen of the sciences, having lost a sense of her
own meaning and integrity, had become a common prostitute" (p. 111),
catering to a series of fads.
34. Michael Novak, "The Enlightenment is Dead," in *The Center Magazine,*
IV (March/April, 1971): 19–20. The title of the article seemed to me to
be contradicted by its content, as the quotations suggest.

American history, "while Protestants pointed with pride to their achievements they hardly realized that the typically rationalist view of the irrelevancy of theological distinctions in a pluralist society was pulling the rug out from under them." And this means, Marty concludes, borrowing a punch line from Oscar Handlin, "that the Enlightenment prevailed over 'the forms American religion took in its development from Calvinism.' "[35] That most of us are closer to the tradition of Enlightenment than to eighteenth-century Christian orthodoxy we realize when we stop to think that we would no doubt find Franklin, Jefferson, Madison, even Thomas Paine more congenial dinner company than Jonathan Edwards, Samuel Davies, George Whitefield, or Timothy Dwight.

Mr. Marty's thesis, noted above, suggests that one might say of most academic theology in America what George Herbert Mead said of Josiah Royce's philosophy, that it "was part of the escape from the crudity of American life, not an interpretation of it," for "it . . . did not root in the active life of the community" and therefore "was not an interpretation of American life." So, Mead continues, although from around 1800 "culture was sought vividly in institutions of learning, in lyceums and clubs, it did not reflect the political and economic activities which were fundamental in American life."[36]

35. Martin E. Marty, *The New Shape of American Religion* (New York: Harper & Bros., 1959), pp. 71–72.
36. George Herbert Mead, "The Philosophies of Royce, James, and Dewey in Their American Setting," in Andrew J. Reck, ed., *Selected Writings of George Herbert Mead* (Indianapolis: Bobbs-Merrill Company's Library of Liberal Arts), 1964. The quotations are, in order, from pages 383, 376, 377, and 381. The essay was first published in the *International Journal of Ethics* 40 (1929-1930): 211–31; it seems to me that George Santayana argued essentially the same thesis in his famous essay on "The Genteel Tradition." Herbert Wallace Schneider spelled out "how philosophy [in America] lost its living connections with the general culture of the American people and became a technical discipline in academic curricula. At the same time . . . religion and morals gradually severed their philosophical bonds, and, as the philosophers would say, became unenlightened." *A History of American Philosophy* (New York: Columbia University Press, 1946), p. 225.

And one might say of Marty's Protestant Christians, un-
aware that the rug was being pulled out from under them
by Enlightenment, what Mead said of William James: "He
was not aware of the break between the profound processes
of American life [Parsons's social system] and its culture
[Parsons's culture system]."[37]

In a most perceptive essay published in 1964, the late
historian-theologian Joseph Haroutunian gave more definite
theological content to the development to which Marty and
Mead pointed. The predominant Christian orthodoxy in the
United States, he argues,

> has been a *tour de force*, which has persisted and flourished
> largely either as a denial of or as an escape from American
> experience. . . . Its supernaturalism and appeal to authority;
> its pitching of Christian doctrine against the ideas of the
> scientific community and its advocacy of faith as against intel-
> ligence; its severing prayer from work and the sacred from
> the secular have made orthodoxy an alien spirit in American
> life and its theology an alien mind in a land which has re-
> warded industry and method with good things and common
> prosperity.[38]

After giving due regard to the liberal and other theological
movements in the United States he summarizes his view in
an understatement: "It appears that American Christianity
has done less than justice to American Experience, and so
have American theologians."

I assume that the theologians are the intellectuals of a
community of faith or belief. I am using the word "intel-
lectual(s)" in the sense developed by Shils and Parsons in
the articles noted above. In Parsons's terminology, the intellectual is "expected . . . to put cultural considerations

37. Mead, "The Philosophies of Royce, James, and Dewey," p. 381.
38. Joseph Haroutunian, "Theology and American Experience," *Criterion*
(Winter, 1964): 7–9. *Criterion* is, or was, the house organ of the Divinity
School of The University of Chicago.

above social," his function being to define and, presumably, to articulate and disseminate the meaning system (or "value orientation") of his society. Shils spelled this out in clearer fashion. He assumed, as noted above, that communities are "bound together by the acceptance of a common body of standards" which are internalized and "continually . . . applied by each member in his own work and in the institutions which assess and select works and persons for appreciation or condemnation." These standards are seldom rationalized and made overt but are carried and maintained primarily in "songs, histories, poems, biographies, and constitutions, etc., which diffuse a sense of affinity among the members of the society."

Intellectuals are driven by a "need to penetrate beyond the screen of immediate concrete experience"—that is, beyond the concerns relative to Parsons's social system—to the "ultimate principles" implicit therein, which is to say "the existing body of cultural values." Then by "preaching, teaching, and writing" in "schools, churches, newspapers, and similar structures" they "infuse into sections of the population which are intellectual neither by inner vocation nor by social role, a perceptiveness and an imagery which they would otherwise lack."[39] Here in Shils's terminology we may recognize James Baldwin's conception of the respon-

---

39. Shils, "The Intellectuals and the Powers," pp. 27–30. Adolf A. Berle, Jr., in his book *Power Without Property: A New Development in American Political Economy* (New York: Harcourt, Harvest Book, 1929; e.g., pp. 90–91, 110–16, and 154–55) makes a helpful distinction between the "public consensus" and the "public opinion" that carries the same connotations as Shils's designation of the role of the intellectual vis-à-vis the general population; Berle's "public consensus" points to Shils's "common standards," and Berle's "public opinion" points to temporary winds of opinion which often run counter to the "public consensus" or the "common standards." In my terminology, developed in articles and unpublished lectures during the past years, the intellectuals define, describe, and teach the elements of the historical "character" of a people who constitute a community, as distinct from the temporary "shapes" their movements may take; A people's conception of their true character is invoked in judgment on their immediate shape.

sibility of the artist-writer to clarify and articulate the hidden laws that govern his society and himself.

I hear Parsons and Shils saying that the task of the intellectuals is to infuse in the population the beliefs and standards that define what is normal behavior in their society, and that these beliefs are legitimated by the ultimate principles implicit in them. This means in my way of speaking that, ideally, intellectuals would assume responsibility for inculcating the religion of their commmunity.

This seems to me essentially the thesis David W. Noble developed in his book, *Historians Against History: The Frontier Thesis and the National Covenant in American Historical Writing Since 1890.* The historian, Noble argues, "is our most important secular theologian," responsible for describing and defending the covenant that makes us a people, being always ready both to "explain how his country has achieved its uniqueness" and to "warn against the intrusion of alien influences."[40]

What I have described as the separation of "salvation" from social responsibility, in the terminology of Parsons and Shils could be described as a separation of the cultural system and value orientation professed in a community from the actual social system, or the divorce of religion from what George Herbert Mead called "the political and economic activities which were fundamental in American life."

Traditionally in Christendom the church, a very tangible institution *in*, but conceived as not entirely *of*, the society,[41]

40. David W. Noble, *Historians Against History: The Frontier Thesis and the National Covenant in American Historical Writing Since 1890.* (Minneapolis: University of Minnesota Press, 1965), pp. 4, 17. Robert N. Bellah, a self-confessed "former establishment fundamentalist," definitely assumes this role in his book, *The Broken Covenant.* His "Confessions of a Former Establishment Fundamentalist" was published in *Bulletin of the Council on the Study of Religion* 1, 3 (December, 1970): 3–6.

41. For this distinction, see Tocqueville's "The Principle of the Sovereignty of the People in America," which is chap. 4 in vol. I, Pt. 1 of his *Democracy in America*; in the translation by George Lawrence, edited by J. P. Mayer and Max Lerner (New York: Harper & Row, 1966), pp. 51–53.

was the home of the intellectuals. The church in this respect was roughly analogous to the university in our society. For those who lived during the centuries of Catholic Christendom, as for the Puritans of early Massachusetts Bay, theologians played the role in society that Parsons and Shils designate as *the* role of intellectuals in any society.[42] Further, they were expected to give guidance to rulers and people, in minute detail if necessary, for they were the recognized interpreters of the proper application of the general standards to specific issues. In this social-cultural structure "salvation" was inextricably bound to right conduct in every area of life from birth to last rites.

With the fragmentation of the transnational church by the Reformation, and the establishment of religious pluralism, this unified authoritarian structure was destroyed and Christianity was thereafter incarnated in many different and highly competitive institutions, each legitimated by its absolutized parochial interpretation of the common gospel. Each Established church that resulted made for its place in its nation the same sort of claims that the universal Catholic church had made for its ubiquitous transnational authority. In other words, the new nations reverted to tribalism, and an Established church was the institutionalization of the nation's tribal cult.

In this situation no substantive difference was made between church and commonwealth. Both were merely ways of looking at the same body of people. This was evidenced in the legal structure by the merging of monarch into God, legitimated by some forms of the doctrine of the divine right of kings.[43] In this context the role of the theologian

42. This seems to be commonly assumed by historians. For example, Edmund S. Morgan says that the founders of New England "knew, from the works of theologians, what principles they must embody in their new institutions." *Roger Williams: the Church and the State* (New York: Harcourt, Brace & World, 1967), p. 68.
43. See John Neville Figgis, *The Divine Right of Kings* (New York: Harper and Row, Torchbooks, 1965), passim.

of an Established church was that of a true intellectual of and for his nation-society.

When the American Revolution was completed, let us say with John Adams by around 1815,[14] not only had the Established Church of England been rejected, but, more important, the very idea of Establishment had been discarded in principle by the new Constitution. For the first time in Christendom there was legal *religious freedom* as distinct from toleration in a commonwealth.[45] Church and

44. Adams wrote in 1815, "The last twenty-five years of the last century, and the first fifteen years of this, may be called the age of revolutions and constitutions." Adams commonly made a distinction between the Revolution and the War for Independence. In 1818 he wrote, "But what do we mean by the American Revolution? Do we mean the American war? The Revolution was effected before the war commenced. The Revolution was in the minds and hearts of the people; a change in their religious sentiments of their duties and obligations." And this Revolution, he thought, might be said to have begun "as early as the first plantation of the country." Adrienne Koch, ed., *The American Enlightenment: The Shaping of the American Experiment and a Free Society* (New York: George Braziller, 1965), pp. 223, 228, 229.

45. Jefferson was very conscious of the distinction, and in this respect quite aware of how he and his fellow Americans differed from Locke. In his "Notes on Religion" written around 1782 Jefferson notes that "Locke denies toleration to those who entertain opinions contrary to those moral rules necessary for the preservation of society, as for instance, that faith is not to be kept with those of another persuasion, that Kings excommunicated forfeit their crowns, that dominion is founded in grace, or that obedience is due to some foreign prince; or who will not own and teach the duty of tolerating all men in matters of religion; or who deny the existence of a god (it was a great thing to go so far—as he himself says of the parliament which framed the act of toleration—but where he stopped short we may go on)." Saul K. Padover, ed., *The Complete Jefferson* (New York: Duell, Sloan & Pearce, Inc., 1943), p. 945.

Adrienne Koch, after quoting this in part, adds: "That he went on, and America went on, from toleration to religious freedom is very much to the point in our general understanding of the American Enlightenment." "Pragmatic Wisdom and the American Enlightenment," *The William and Mary Quarterly* 18, 3 (July 1961): 323.

It seems generally agreed that the American leaders' ideas were not original. Herbert W. Schneider in his *A History of American Philosophy* (p. 36), asserts that they "had no systems of thought, and they consciously borrowed most of the scattered ideas which they put into action." One cannot, he argued, "make the American Enlightenment appear as a 'glorious revolution' in thought as well as in fact."

It seems equally agreed that the Americans differed from European think-

state could no longer be seen as coextensive functional institutionalized authorities—as merely two ways of looking at the same society. A church became a voluntary association within the commonwealth, in competition with perhaps hundreds of others. Loyalty to God, symbol of the highest ideals and standards (cultural system), could now be distinguished from loyalty to monarch or state, symbols of nation (social system), and it was possible to conceive that the two might be in conflict. This development is what John Adams meant by "the Revolution"—the change that took place "in the minds and hearts of the people" which he described as "a change in their religious sentiments of their duties and obligations."[46]

With this Revolution the theologian, who had lost his transnational perspective with the Reformation, lost also his national perspective, and became the intellectual for but one of the multitude of competing sects. Now his primary role was to construct a solid defense of his sect's peculiar species of Christianity against all the other sects making the same absolutistic claim. Because the one thing all Christians held in common was the authority of Scripture, all such defenses were erected on this foundation. This meant that even while ostensibly defending the authority of the Bible against sceptics, infidels, and atheists, each sect was actually contending against all other Christian groups for sole possession of the revelation by right of having the only, or most nearly, correct interpretation of it. Meantime the Revolution

---

ers because of their practical political experience and their unique opportunity to put the revolutionary ideas into practice. This is stressed by Hannah Arendt (*On Revolution* [New York: Viking Press, 1965], pp. 115–16), who argues that "compared to this American experience, the preparation of the French *hommes de lettres* who were to make the Revolution was theoretical in the extreme. . . . They had no experience to fall back upon, only ideas and principles untested by reality."

Adrienne Koch stresses the same point in the Introduction to her *The American Enlightenment*, pp. 19–45.

46. Letter to H. Niles, February 13, 1818, in Koch, *The American Enlightenment*, p. 228.

meant that all their sectarian claims had been made completely irrelevant to the individual's status and rights as a
citizen, and to the being and well-being of the commonwealth in which they lived. Thus the competition between
the sects undermined belief in the distinctive beliefs of all
of them. For in the minds of Mr. and Ms. John Q. Public
the strident claims of the sects simply cancelled each other
out, as their Republic was teaching them that no sect's distinctives had a bearing on their rights as citizens.[47]

Meantime the new kind of commonwealth that had
emerged in Christendom found cosmic legitimation in Enlightenment theology—the cosmopolitan perspective that
induced Benamin Franklin to pray that God would "grant,
that not only the Love of Liberty, but a thorough Knowledge of the Rights of Man, may pervade all the Nations of
the Earth, so that a Philosopher may set his Foot anywhere
on its Surface, and say, 'This is my Country.' "[48]

The same sentiment prompted Alexander Hamilton to
suggest in the first Federalist Paper that in the new kind of
nation being born philanthropy (love for mankind) must
always temper patriotism (love for country), which is to say
that "national security" is not necessarily always the ultimate consideration.

It was this cosmopolitan theology that the Christian
denominations almost universally rejected during the course
of the revivals that swept across the nation following the
1790s. In doing so they turned back to pre-eighteenth-
century theologians, or to the theologians of Europe's
Established churches, for the framework of their intellectual
structures, while the meaning system that informed and
legitimated the social, economic, political, and judicial systems of the nation followed in the tradition of Enlightenment thinking.[49] It was this development that institution-

47. The case of Lucy Mack Smith, mother of the prophet, Joseph Smith,
illustrates this.
48. Franklin's letter to David Hartley, December 4, 1789, in Koch, *The
American Enlightenment,* p. 107.

alized the separation of "salvation" from the convert's responsibility for the structures of his society.[50]

One of the most extensively documented historical generalizations is that Enlightenment was driven underground by social opprobrium and character assassination of the infidel, but that its meaning system (to use Parsons' terms) was never examined for its intellectual merits and refuted by Christian theologians.[51] The Enlightenment meaning system continued, of course, to have its more or less able defenders. But most of them might rightly complain with Thomas Paine that his Christian opponents confounded "a dispute about authenticity with a dispute about doctrines," that is, in answer to his questioning of the authority of the Bible as sole revelation of God for teaching man his duty, they quoted Scripture to refute him.[52] This suggests what I suspect was the case, that the great majority of clerical leaders and theologians did not recognize the real issue or realize the nature of the revolution in thinking that was taking place. Each in his denominational stockade tended to absolutize and universalize his parochial species of Christianity, while sharing with those in his Christian opponents' ghettoes the common abhorrence of "infidelity." The "infidel" was on everyone's enemies list.[53]

49. In making this point in class lectures Professor Wilhelm Pauck used to tell us that modern man stands either with one foot in the Reformation and the other on a banana peel, or with one foot in the Enlightenment and the other on the banana peel. I suppose that the two most prestigious representatives of the Reformation and the Enlightenment in my day were Karl Barth and Albert Schweitzer respectively.

50. See n. 29.

51. This was extensively spelled out in my *Nathaniel William Taylor: A Connecticut Liberal* (Chicago: University of Chicago Press, 1942), Chapters IV and VI. More recent literature is noted in the article by Mary Kelley and myself, "Protestantism in the Shadow of Enlightenment," in *Soundings*, 58, 3 (Fall 1975): 345, n. 42.

52. Thomas Paine, *The Age of Reason*, preface to Part II.

53. See Martin E. Marty, *The Infidel: Free Thought and American Religion* (Cleveland: World Pub. Co.'s Meridian Books, 1961), passim, for delineation of how the image of "the infidel" was often created and universally used by Christian leaders in America to rally support for their enterprises by pointing to a common enemy.

This meant, to repeat my thesis, that every ardent defense of sectarian Christianity, however unintentional, was by implication an attack on the mainspring of the Republic.[54] Consequently the intellectuals—the unofficial "theologians" of the Republic—explaining, defending, acting upon, and infusing the values of the commonwealth were commonly anathema to the leaders of institutionalized Christianity. Either that or—and this was done by Robert Baird, who published his *Religion in America* in 1844–45—they were posthumously metamorphosed into his species of good sectarian Christians.[55]

54. A striking example of this effect was noted in *Liberty* 58 (November-December, 1963): 8–9. In the state of Hawaii Christmas and Good Friday were paid holidays for state employees; they cost the state about $500,000 a year. In February of 1963 a state senator introduced two bills into the Hawaiian Legislature. The first would have removed Christmas and Good Friday from the list of *paid* holidays. The second, an alternate bill, would have added a "Buddha Day" (April 8) to the paid holidays at an additional cost of about $250,000. It would seem, granted the large Buddhist population, that either bill would have been fair, and in principle compatible with the Court's interpretation of the First Amendment. But in reaction to the proposed legislation Protestant Billy Graham declared, "If we take away these days [Christmas and Good Friday] we are taking away the basis of our way of life, our religion"; and a Roman Catholic Monsignor asserted, "The state of Hawaii and the other forty-nine states ought to be amazed at the arrogance of those who insult God-fearing people by stamping out the traditional observance of the greatest Christian feast of the year." Obviously neither bill, if passed, would have *taken away* or *stamped out* either Christmas or Good Friday. What both of these highly visible Christian leaders were actually contending for was continued recognition and support by the civil authority of their particular species of Christianity against all other religious faiths—a direct attack on the principle of religious freedom inherent in the First Amendment.

55. H. Richard Niebuhr is an example of a very honest, tender, and sensitive person and most able thinker impaled on the horns of the dilemma posed by the Christian absolutism he inherited and defended in his denomination and the relativism of the pluralistic cosmopolitan society in which he came to live as a Yale professor. In him the problem was personified of how to be an absolutist in a relativistic and cosmopolitan world; or, vocationally, how to be a theologian for a particular species of Christianity while serving as a professorial intellectual at pluralistic Yale. My impression is that a majority of professors in the "liberal" theological schools circumvent this problem by quietly renouncing responsibility for and to the denomination with which they may be at least nominally affiliated. H. Richard Niebuhr was made of sterner mental and spiritual stuff, so in his writings the tension is made manifest.

This development meant the emergence in the common-wealth of two disparate, even competing culture systems, inculcating different conceptions of a proper social system, each with its own kind of intellectuals. Many theologians of the sects continued to talk as if they were the exponents of the normative culture system of the commonwealth, while actually they represented only that of, at best Christianity in general, at worst their exclusive sect. Meantime the intellectuals of the commonwealth, e.g., Jefferson, Franklin, Lincoln, and even Eisenhower, naturally found no real religious home in any existing sect. And many sensitive persons squirmed to have the best of both worlds, usually in the end by giving each a separate but equal compartment in their minds.

The question of the place of sectarian theologians in the commonwealth was solved by default. For with the general erosion of belief noted above, they lost even their vocation as defenders of what the Parson Thwackums among them have called denominational distinctives against both those of the other Christian sects and unbelievers. They became, at their best, defenders of the theologically amorphous but highly moralistic species of Christianity-in-general represented in recent decades by *The Christian Century*, at their worst pugnacious and powerful sectarian isolationists like the Rev. Carl McIntire. In either case, having usually been programmed in their theological schools to confuse the cosmopolitan Enlightenment theology with worship of the state, they have found it hard to find a plausibly significant role to play in the society.[56]

56. Herbert W. Schneider noted the metamorphosis of the eighteenth-century type of philosopher who was an investigator, either natural or moral, into "the nineteenth-century . . . species of educator known as professors of philosophy" who "were primarily teachers" whose "ambition was to be orthodox, to teach the truth, i.e., to instruct their students in correct doctrine. . . . Similarly," Schneider adds, "the theologians lost most of their speculative or philosophical interest and were content to refine their systems for the edification of the faithful and the confounding of rival theologians. In short, our history of American philosophy now takes us into the schoolrooms of colleges and seminaries. What President Francis Wayland

54		*Religion and the American Revolution*

George Santayana described the fanatic as one who re-
doubles his efforts when he has lost his aim. This is an apt
characterization of the faddishness that has characterized
professional theology during the past several decades.[57] It
is not surprising, when seen in this context, that as long ago
as 1933, theological school professor John C. Bennett la-
mented a widespread "feeling of theological homelessness"
among his kind.[58]

---

said of his own famous textbook in moral science states the idea of orthodoxy in general: 'Being designed for the purposes of instruction, its aim is
to be simple, clear, and purely didactic.' " *A History of American Philosophy*, p. 226.

Alfred North Whitehead concluded that "theology has largely failed" in
its function "to provide a rational understanding of the rise of civilization,
and of the tenderness of mere life itself, in a world which superficially is
founded upon the clashings of senseless compulsion," and stated his belief
that "the defect of the liberal theology of the last two hundred years is that
it has confined itself to the suggestion of minor, vapid reasons why people
should continue to go to church in the traditional fashion." *Adventures
of Ideas* (New York: The Free Press, 1967), p. 170.

More devastating was the curt comment of top-flight theologian John B.
Cobb, Jr., in 1967 that, while "there is no lack of highly trained and intelligent men keenly interested in constructive theological work," their "essays
for the most part are trivial" and leave "a vacuum in which even the splash
of a small pebble attracts widespread attention"—and, he should have
added, only in the very restricted circle of the jet-set professorial theologians outside of which the attention attracted seems to be practically nil.
"From Crisis Theology to the Post-Modern World," in Bernard Murchland,
ed., *The Meaning of the Death of God: Protestant, Jewish and Catholic
Scholars Explore Atheistic Theology* (New York: Vintage Books, 1967), p.
138.

57. See Mary Kelley and Sidney E. Mead, "Protestantism in the Shadow of
Enlightenment," pp. 338–42.

58. John C. Bennett, "After Liberalism—What?" *The Christian Century* 50
(November 8, 1933): 1403.

ROBERT N. BELLAH

THE REVOLUTION AND THE
CIVIL RELIGION

There is a sense in which the American Revolution and the American civil religion are the same thing. When I use the term "civil religion" I am pointing to that revolution in the minds of men that John Adams argued was the real Revolution in America. That was the revolution that culminated in the Declaration of Independence, even though the Revolutionary War had scarcely begun.

It is that Revolutionary faith—what Lincoln called "our ancient faith"—that I have called the American civil religion, or at least its normative core. In order that there be no ambiguity about what I mean I would like to cite briefly the Declaration of Independence, and also the Gettysburg Address which represents a rededication to and renewal of that primary text:

> When in the course of human events, it becomes necessary for one people to dissolve the political bands which have connected them with another, and to assume among the powers of the earth the separate and equal station to which the Laws of Nature and of Nature's God entitle them, a decent respect to the opinions of mankind requires that they should declare the causes which impel them to the separation.—We hold these truths to be self-evident, that all men are created equal, that they are endowed by their creator with certain unalienable rights, that among these are life, liberty and the pursuit of happiness.—That to secure these rights, governments are instituted among men, deriving their just powers from the consent of the governed.

And from the Gettysburg Address the opening and the closing statements:

> Four score and seven years ago our fathers brought forth on this continent, a new nation, conceived in Liberty, and dedicated to the proposition that all men are created equal. . . . It is rather for us to be here dedicated to the great task remaining before us— . . . that this nation, under God, shall have a new birth of freedom—and that government of the people, by the people, for the people, shall not perish from the earth.

It is that abstract faith, those abstract propositions to which we are dedicated, that is the heart and soul of the civil religion; but we can, of course, never forget the historical circumstances in which those words originated—a revolutionary war of independence and a war to decide whether this nation would be slave or free. While there are many other embellishments, symbols, traditions, and interpretations that have become more or less securely part of the American civil religion, I think we already have before us the fundamental form of its faith. The words are so familiar that they have become for many almost empty of meaning. But their meaning has never been more critical for testing the condition of the political society in which we live.

In defining the American civil religion there was a certain ambiguity in my original article[1] that I would now like to clear up. In that article I pointed to those classic documents that unmistakably define the special character of the American faith, the documents from which I have just quoted. But in taking the term "civil religion" from Rousseau's *Social Contract* I was also bringing in a much more general concept, common in America in the eighteenth century but

1. Robert N. Bellah, "Civil Religion in America," *Daedalus,* Winter 1967. Reprinted in Robert N. Bellah, *Beyond Belief: Essays on Religion in a Post-Traditional World* (New York: Harper and Row, 1970).

by no means specifically American. Therefore I think it might be useful to distinguish between two different types of civil religion, both operative in America and distinguishable perhaps more in the minds of the analyst than in the consciousness of the people. These two types I would like to call special civil religion, that which I have just defined, and general civil religion, which I would now like to describe.

It is the essence of general civil religion that it is religion in general, the lowest common denominator of church religions. Though religion in general and lowest common denominator religion were attacked in the fifties as a modern perversion of traditional religion by neoorthodox critics and those like Will Herberg who were influenced by them, actually such general religion has a long and honorable history in Christendom. It is what was called natural religion. And natural religion was generally agreed for many centuries to be an indispensable prerequisite for government. Roger Williams, for example, for all his insistence on the separation of church and state, believed that such general religion was essential for what he called "government and order in families, towns, etc." Such general religion is, he believed, "written in the hearts of all mankind, yea, even in pagans," and consists in belief in God, in the afterlife, and in divine punishments.[2] Benjamin Franklin for all his differences from Roger Williams believed essentially the same thing, as indicated in the quotation from his autobiography in my original article on civil religion. Elsewhere Franklin emphasized the importance of general religion when he wrote, "If men are so wicked as we now see them *with religion*, what would they be *without it?*"[3]

2. Roger Williams to Daniel Abbot, January 15, 1681, in Edmund S. Morgan, ed., *Puritan Political Ideas* (Indianapolis: The Bobbs-Merrill Co., 1965), p. 224.
3. Ralph Ketcham, ed., *The Political Thought of Benjamin Franklin* (Indianapolis: The Bobbs-Merrill Co., 1965), p. 144.

But the classic expression of general civil religion is surely to be found in George Washington's Farewell Address:

> Of all the suppositions and habits which lead to political prosperity, Religion and morality are indispensable supports. In vain would that man claim the tribute of Patriotism, who should labour to subvert these great Pillars of human happiness, these firmest props of the duties of Men and citizens. The mere Politician, equally with the pious man ought to respect and cherism them. A volume could not trace all their connections with private and public felicity. Let it simply be asked where is the security for property, for reputation, for life, if the sense of religious obligation desert the oaths, which are the instruments of investigation in Courts of Justice? And let us with caution indulge the supposition, that morality can be maintained without religion. Whatever may be conceded to the influence of refined education on minds of peculiar structure, reason and experience both forbid us to expect that National morality can prevail in exclusion of religious principle.[4]

And a little later in the address he asks, "Can it be, that Providence has not connected the permanent felicity of a Nation with its virtue?"[5]

It is these statements, I believe, that foreshadow the famous and much criticized remark of Dwight David Eisenhower, "Our government makes no sense unless it is founded in a deeply felt religious faith—and I don't care what it is."[6] Being charitable to Eisenhower I think we may doubt that he didn't care *at all*: he meant he didn't care *which* of the conventional American religious faiths it was because all of them have the requisite minimal features of general civil religion. Supreme Court Justice William O. Douglas, a man on the opposite side of the political fence

4. Saxe Cummins, ed., *The Basic Writings of George Washington* (New York: Random House, 1948), p. 637.
5. Ibid., p. 638.
6. Dwight D. Eisenhower, in Will Herbert, *Protestant-Catholic-Jew* (Garden City, N.Y.: Doubleday and Co., 1955), p. 97.

from Eisenhower, said much the same thing in a 1952 Supreme Court decision when he wrote, "We are a religious people whose institutions presuppose a Supreme Being."[7]

We should not assume, however, that all Americans from the seventeenth century on have been quite so inclusive with respect to general civil religion. Williams, Franklin, and Washington were willing to accept Catholics and Jews along with Protestants, and Williams was ready to include Muslims as well. Indeed some of the noblest sentiments of inclusion in the common fellowship in our history are to be found in the letters and addresses of Washington to religious organizations. Particularly remarkable are his sentiments of strong acceptance and support of groups that have sometimes been considered marginal by many Americans: Roman Catholics, for example, or Quakers. But the high point in these letters and addresses is certainly the Address to the Hebrew Congregation of New Port on August 17, 1790, well known to Jewish Americans but not so familiar to many of us:

> The citizens of the United States of America have a right to applaud themselves for having given to Mankind examples of an enlarged and liberal policy, a policy worthy of imitation. All possess alike liberty of conscience and immunities of citizenship. It is now no more that toleration is spoken of, as if it was by the indulgence of one class of people, that another enjoyed the exercise of their inherent natural rights. For happily the Government of the United States, which gives to bigotry no sanction, to persecution no assistance, requires only that they who live under its protection should demean themselves as good citizens, in giving it on all occasions their effectual support. . . .
>
> May the children of the Stock of Abraham, who dwell in this land, continue to merit and enjoy the good will of the

7. Zorach v. Clauson, 343 U.S. 306 (1952), 312–313. Cited in Mark De-Wolfe Howe, *The Garden and the Wilderness: Religion and Government in American Constitutional History* (Chicago: The University of Chicago Press, 1965), p. 13.

other inhabitants, while every one shall sit in safety under his own vine and fig tree, and there shall be none to make him afraid.[8]

But it was a long and slow process before Catholics and Jews were fully included in our civil consensus. Mark De Wolf Howe and William McLoughlin have argued that there was a de facto Protestant establishment in the early years of the Republic, that this establishment was broadened to include Catholics late in the nineteenth century and that only in the twentieth has America transcended the notion that it is a Christian nation. In any case the idea that religion is the basis of public morality, and so the indispensable underpinning of a republican political order, is a constant theme from Washington's Farewell Address to the present. This fundamental function of general civil religion could be carried out by churches that remained indifferent to the special civil religion embodied in such documents as the Declaration of Independence and bound up with the history of the American nation, but most American religious groups have been able to affirm both general and special civil religion as well as their own doctrinal peculiarities. In this fusion Protestant denominations have been joined by Catholics and Jews almost to the present.

The founding fathers believed that religion and morality were the essential basis for that virtue which Washington said Providence always connects with the felicity of a nation. But how hopeful were they that virtue, the very principle of a republic, would survive in America? Our founding fathers, children of the eighteenth century though they might be, were not callow optimists. Washington in his Farewell Address wrote that he dared not hope that his

8. George Washington, in Paul F. Boller, Jr., *George Washington and Religion* (Dallas: Southern Methodist University Press, 1963), p. 186.

counsels could "prevent our Nation from running the course which has hitherto marked the Destiny of Nations."[9]

What that course was Franklin made clear in his speech on the very last day of the Constitutional Convention, September 17, 1787:

> In these sentiments, Sir, I agree to this Constitution with all its faults, if they are such; because I think a general Government necessary for us, and there is no form of Government but what may be a blessing to the people if well administered, and believe further that this is likely to be well administered for a course of years, and can only end in Despotism, as other forms have done before it, when the people shall have become so corrupted as to need despotic Government, being incapable of any other.[10]

These sentiments are amplified in an earlier letter written in 1775 to Joseph Priestly:

> It will scarce be credited in Britain, that men can be as diligent with us from zeal for the public good, as with you for thousands per annum. Such is the difference between uncorrupted new states, and corrupted old ones.[11]

And Jefferson parallels Washington and Franklin in his "Notes on Virginia," 1781:

> The spirit of the times may alter, will alter. Our rulers will become corrupt, our people careless. A single zealot may commence persecutor, and better men be his victims. It can never be too often repeated, that the time for fixing every essential right on a legal basis is while our rulers are honest, and ourselves united. From the conclusion of this war we shall be going down hill. It will not then be necessary to resort every moment to the people for support. They will

9. Cummins, *Basic Writings of George Washington*, p. 642.
10. Ketcham, *Political Thought of Benjamin Franklin*, p. 401.
11. Ibid., p. 288.

62   *Religion and the American Revolution*

be forgotten, therefore, and their rights disregarded. They
will forget themselves, but in the sole faculty of making
money, and will never think of uniting to effect a due respect
for their rights. The shackles, therefore, which shall not be
knocked off at the conclusion of this war, will remain on us
long, will be made heavier and heavier, till our rights shall
revive or expire in a convulsion.[12]

If we ask what virtue and corruption meant to the founding fathers the answer is clear from the quotations I have
just cited and from many more I could have cited. Franklin described it as "zeal for the public good." Jefferson put
it a little differently when he described virtue as "a love of
others, a sense of duty to them, a moral instinct, in short,
which prompts us irresistably to feel and to succor their dis-
tresses."[13] Corruption is the opposite of "zeal for the
public good." It is exclusive concern for one's own good,
for, in Franklin's words, "thousands per annum." For
Jefferson, corruption consists in forgetting oneself "in the
sole faculty of making money."

If we can see the connection between general civil religion and virtue defined as concern for the common good, we
can begin to see the connections between general civil religion and special civil religion, for special civil religion
defines the norms in terms of which the common good is
conceived. Perhaps the central norm in the American civil
religion is expressed in that great phrase of Jefferson in the
Declaration of Independence: "All men are created equal."
But it is widely asserted that the founding fathers were
hypocrites, that Jefferson didn't really mean it. I recently
heard it said on a television discussion that since Jefferson
believed in slavery he meant "all men are created equal" to

12. Thomas Jefferson, "Notes on Virginia," Query 17, in Saul K. Padover,
ed., *The Complete Jefferson* (New York: Duell, Sloan & Pearce, 1943), p.
676.
13. Thomas Jefferson to Thomas Law, June 13, 1814, cited in John R.
Howe, Jr., *The Changing Political Thought of John Adams* (Princeton:
Princeton University Press, 1966), p. 31.

apply only to whites; nor was that view contradicted by any member of the distinguished panel. Silly adulation of the George Washington and the cherry tree variety is certainly to be abhorred, but silly debunking is no improvement. As a matter of fact Jefferson never believed in slavery, always argued that it was wrong, consistently tried to limit and contain it so that it could eventually be suppressed, and— what anyone talking on the subject of the Declaration of Independence should know—condemned it utterly in his own draft of that document. One of the charges against the king of England that was unfortunately struck out by Congress read in Jefferson's original words:

> He has waged cruel war against human nature itself, violating its most sacred rights of life and liberty in the persons of a distant people, who never offended him, captivating and carrying them into slavery in another hemisphere, or to incur miserable death in their transportation thither.[14]

In his *Summary View of the Rights of British America* of 1774 Jefferson had called for the "abolition of domestic slavery" and the eventual "enfranchisement of the slaves we have."[15] In his "Notes on Virginia" of 1781 Jefferson foresaw a future "total emancipation" but was not insensitive to the irony of a people fighting for its own freedom keeping another in subjection. He placed the issue of slavery in the light that Abraham Lincoln would always see it when he wrote in 1781:

> And can the liberties of a nation be thought secure when we have removed their only firm basis, a conviction in the minds of the people that their liberties are of the gift of God—that they are not to be violated but with His wrath? Indeed I tremble for my country when I reflect that God is just; that his justice cannot sleep forever; that, considering numbers, nature, and natural means only, a revolution of the wheel of

14. Padover, *The Complete Jefferson*, p. 32.
15. Ibid., p. 14.

fortune, an exchange of situation [between masters and slaves] is among the possible events; that it may become probable by supernatural interference! The Almighty has no attribute which can take sides with us in such a contest.[16]

Jefferson, unlike Lincoln, did not often resort to biblical language, but the injustice of slavery called it forth in him. One cannot but see those words as a foreshadowing of Lincoln's great Second Inaugural Address:

> Yet if God wills that [this war] continue until all the wealth piled up by the bondsmen's two hundred and fifty years of unrequited toil shall be sunk, and every drop of blood drawn with the lash shall be paid by another drawn by the sword, as was said three thousand years ago, so still it must be said "the judgments of the Lord are true and righteous altogether."

There is, then, a biting edge to the civil religion. Not just general civil religion, but virtue. Not just virtue, but concern for the common good. Not just the common good defined in any self-serving way, but the common good under great objective norms: equality, life, liberty, the pursuit of happiness.

The American civil religion could not guarantee the instant fulfillment of its precepts. No religion has ever been able so to guarantee. Do all Christians love their neighbors as themselves? The world, as Christians have long known and as the founding fathers certainly knew, is a wicked place. Compromise with existing evil is necessary for survival. But religions have a way of going beyond necessary compromise and tacitly condoning or even supporting evil when it could be effectively opposed. I would not deny that the civil religion has been used to condone evil, any more than I would deny that Christians have used their

16. *Notes on Virginia,* Query 18, in Padover, *The Complete Jefferson,* p. 677.

religion to condone evil. And yet the fundamental tenets of the civil religion have continued to work among us. How different our history would have been if the Declaration of Independence had read, "All white people are created equal and all black people are created slaves by nature."

I have concentrated on slavery because it has occasioned the deepest moral and political trauma in our history. A tragic civil war was required to abolish it, and its effects are still far from eradicated today. But slavery is only an image, an emblem, an example of the more general problem: how to actualize on this earth the great religious and moral insights that have been given to us.

I have spoken so far as though the tenets of the civil religion are self-evident, as though they need no interpretation, as though the only problem is their implementation. Actually that is far from the case. Conflict, explicit or implicit, over the deeper meaning of the civil religion has been endemic from the beginning. The conflict over the meaning of the civil religion, over the very meaning of American, has never been more severe than it is today,[17] and how we as a people make the great decisions that lie ahead may depend on how we resolve that conflict of meaning.

To put it—for the sake of argument—a bit too simply: there have been behind the civil religion from the beginning two great structures of interpretation, the one I shall call biblical, the other utilitarian. The biblical interpretation stands, above all, under the archetype of the covenant, but it is also consonant with the classical theory of natural law

17. On February 10, 1976, James Kilpatrick, former speechwriter for a former president, declared in a column published in the San Francisco Chronicle that the phrase "all men are created equal" is a "palpable falsehood." In an Associated Press dispatch of September 13, 1975, it was reported that Vice President Nelson A. Rockefeller had declared that the "Judaeo-Christian heritage" is at odds with "free enterprise" and that too much charity may destroy the country. "One of the problems in this country is that we have the Judeo-Christian heritage of wanting to help those in need," the Vice President is quoted as saying.

as derived from ancient philosophy and handed down by the church fathers. The utilitarian interpretation stands, above all, under the archetype of the social contract and is consonant with the modern theory of natural rights as derived from John Locke. The meaning of every key term in the civil religion—certainly liberty and the pursuit of happiness, but also equality and even life—differs in those two perspectives.[18]

As an expression of the biblical archetype that stands behind the civil religion let me turn to that great initial sermon of John Winthrop, "A Model of Christian Charity," delivered on board ship before the landing in Massachusetts in 1630. This sermon was designed to sketch the religious and ethical foundation of the new society the colonists were to build:

From hence wee may frame these Conclusions.

1. first all true Christians are of one body in Christ 1 Cor. 12. 12. 13. 17. [27.] Ye are the body of Christ and members of [your?] parte.

21y. The ligamentes of this body which knitt together are love.

31y. Noe body can be perfect which wants its propper ligamentes.

41y. All the partes of this body being thus united are made soe contiguous in a speciall relacion as they must needes partake of each others strength and infirmity, joy, and sorrowe, weal and woe. 1 Cor: 12, 26. If one member suffers all suffer with it, if one be in honour, all rejoyce with it.

51y. This sensiblenes and Sympathy of each others Condicions will necessarily infuse into each parte a native desire and endeavour, to strengthen defend preserve and comfort the other.

18. A more developed treatment of these contrasts will be found in Robert N. Bellah, *The Broken Covenant: American Civil Religion in Time of Trial* (New York: Seabury Press, 1975).

To insist a little on this Conclusion being the product of all the former the truthe hereof will appeare both by precept and patterne i. John. 3. 10. ye ought to lay downe your lives for the brethren Gal: 6.2. beare ye one anothers burthens and soe fulfill the lawe of Christ.[19]

Only a little further in the sermon he adds:

The next consideration is how this love comes to be wrought; Adam in his first estate was a perfect modell of mankinde in all theire generacions, and in him this love was perfected in regard of the habit, but Adam Rent in himselfe from his Creator, rent all his posterity alsoe one from another, whence it comes that every man is borne with this principle in him, to love and seeke himselfe onely and thus a man continueth till Christ comes and takes possession of the soule, and infuseth another principle love to God and our brother.[20]

In Winthrop, then, there is a great tension between the situation of fallen men, whose disobedience to God rends them also from each other so that they love themselves alone, and the truly Christian community where all are one body in mutual love and concern. The whole Puritan project was an effort to overcome the failings of fallen or natural man and create a holy community based on love. In an effort to actualize the biblical commandments Winthrop and his friends sought to create a holy commonwealth in England, and if not there then in America. The moral and religious fervor at the root of that effort was the source of much that is good in American society ever since, but we must not forget its dark side: the moral crusade, the holy war, what Paul Tillich called the sin of religion, to confuse one's own will with the will of God. And Winthrop, for all his moderation and humanity, did display that dark side as when several times he turned persecutor and drove religious dissidents from the Bay Colony.

19. Morgan, *Puritan Political Ideas*, pp. 84–86.
20. Ibid., p. 86.

Partly in reaction against the Puritans the great founders of modern philosophy in England, Hobbes and Locke, created a position that was in a sense the dialectical opposite of that of the Puritans. Disturbed by sectarian fanaticism, finding the Puritan goal utopian and finally destructive because, they thought, unrealistic about human nature, they drastically lowered the moral demand, abandoned the principles of Christian politics, and started with natural man, the fallen man of Winthrop, the man who loves himself alone. Thus when, over fifty years after Winthrop's sermon, John Locke discusses the purpose or the end of government he finds it to be not love, as Winthrop would have said, nor justice, as Aristotle would have said, but:

> The great and *chief end* therefore, of Mens uniting into Commonwealths, and putting themselves under Government, *is the Preservation of their Property.*[21]

Or again:

> The commonwealth seems to me to be a society of men constituted only for the procuring, preserving, and advancing their own civil interests.
>   Civil interests I call life, liberty, health, and indolency of body; and the possession of outward things, such as money, lands, houses, furniture, and the like.[22]

Now one can read the great tenets of the civil religion in either of the two perspectives—as Winthrop would have read them, or as Locke would have read them. Is equality a condition for the fulfillment of our humanity in covenant with God or is it a condition for the competitive struggle to attain our own interests? Is freedom almost identical with virtue—the freedom to fulfill lovingly our obligations to

21. John Locke, *The Second Treatise of Government*, paragraph 124.
22. John Locke, *A Letter Concerning Toleration* (Indianapolis: The Bobbs-Merrill Co., 1950), p. 17.

God and our fellow men—or is it the right to do whatever we please so long as we do not harm our fellow men too flagrantly? Is the pursuit of happiness the realization of our true humanity in love of Being and all beings, as Jonathan Edwards[23] would have put it or is it, as Locke would contend, the pursuit of those things—notably wealth and power —which are means to future happiness, in Leo Strauss's words, "The joyless quest for joy"?[24] Does life mean biological survival in our animal functions or does it mean the good life in which our spiritual nature and our animal nature are both fulfilled?

It would simplify matters if Christians had consistently followed what I am calling the biblical interpretation of our civil religion, and deists and rationalists had followed the utilitarian interpretation. Such was not, however, the case. Not only have Christians been on both sides of the fence but we can find the same cleavage in the Enlightenment thought of the founding fathers. The stress on virtue that we have already noticed—Jefferson's "love of others," Franklin's "zeal for the public good"—is very close to the biblical archetype, while the stress on self-interest that is also common among the founding fathers suggests the powerful influence of the utilitarian archetype.

I would argue that it is the idea of virtue that was the organizing center of that initial Revolution in the minds of men that I have identified with the civil religion, the very spirit of the Declaration of Independence. Although in Jefferson the utilitarian side is never absent, the idea of virtue is never eclipsed by the idea of interest. Others of the founding fathers were less constant. Adams's great enthusiasm for virtue during the Revolutionary War turned to scepticism and a reliance on interest in the following

23. Jonathan Edwards, *The Nature of True Virtue,* (Ann Arbor: The University of Michigan Press, 1960).
24. Leo Strauss, *Natural Right and History* (Chicago: The University of Chicago Press, 1953), p. 251.

decade.[25]   Hamilton was never more than mildly intoxi-
cated with the idea of virtue and rapidly became the greatest theorist of the interest-conception of the Republic.[26]
Though most in the founding generation kept some balance
between the two sides, there was a perceptible swing toward
interest by the end of the 1780s. Indeed, if we can say
that virtue is the spirit of the Declaration of Independence,
then interest is the principle of the Constitution. Between
the two documents there is a great lowering of the moral
sights. Madison, who was very much himself of two minds
on the subject of virtue and interest, nonetheless gave the
clearest exposition of the interest-doctrine in the 51st
Federalist:

> Ambition must be made to counteract ambition. The interest
> of the man must be connected with the constitutional rights
> of the place. It may be a reflection on human nature, that
> such devices should be necessary to control the abuses of
> government. But what is government itself, but the greatest
> of all reflections on human nature? If men were angels, no
> government would be necessary. If angels were to govern
> men, neither external nor internal controls on government
> would be necessary. . . .
>   This policy of supplying, by opposite and rival interests,
> the defect of better motives, might be traced through the
> whole system of human affairs, private as well as public. We
> see it particularly displayed in all the subordinate distribu-
> tions of power, where the constant aim is to divide and ar-
> range the several offices in such a manner as that each may
> be a check on the other—that the private interest of every
> individual may be a sentinel over the public rights.[27]

There were several references to God in the Declaration
but none in the Constitution. The Constitution was a

---

25. See Howe, The Garden and the Wilderness, chaps. 2 through 6.
26. See Gerald Stourzh, Alexander Hamilton and the Idea of Republican
Government, (Stanford: University Press, 1970), chap. 2.
27. The Federalist (New York: Modern Library, 1937), p. 158.

document of compromise, as it had to be. Powerful interests had to be taken into account, even when they violated the spirit of the Declaration. It was therefore a document of potential tragedy, as Madison, its chief architect, well knew when he wondered how well it resolved or failed to resolve the problem of slavery. Franklin's words spoken on the last day of the Constitutional Convention and quoted above express the somewhat somber mood. Jefferson's words already quoted, that the "shackles not knocked off" would lead to a "convulsion," proved prophetic, for the shackles of slavery were not knocked off and the seeds of the Civil War were sown from the moment the Constitution was ratified.

I do not mean to say that I think the Constitution was a counterrevolutionary document or that it marked a Thermidorean reaction. It is itself one of the greatest political documents ever produced, one that has stood up incredibly well through nearly two hundred years of enormous social change. But if we can see it as the body of which the Declaration of Independence is the soul then we must see that it was a very imperfect body from the beginning. Almost the first act of the new government was to amend it ten times. It was not until the great Civil War amendments that slavery was finally abolished and the promise of "equal protection of the laws" was made—a promise that has not yet been kept. It was not until the twentieth century that the equality the Declaration promised to all human beings—for that is what "men" meant in the fundamental phrase—began to be fully extended to females as well as males. And the Constitution will undoubtedly have to be changed again in the future if it is to reflect more adequately the truth of its soul. Yet the Constitution was not a betrayal of the Declaration but the inevitable compromise that was necessary if the Declaration was to be incarnated at all.

Thus we have it—virtue and interest, covenant and utili-

tarianism—the American civil religion has always ranged
between those heights and those depths. I would not deny
it. Generations of believing Christians have seen it in its
highest light, though often on Monday morning in the
counting house they have seen it at its lowest. Some of our
greatest leaders, Jefferson and Lincoln included, though
profoundly influenced by modern philosophy, have risen to
a biblical level of insight in our times of need. On the
other hand Christianity has been profoundly infected with
the utilitarian spirit, the primary stress on property and
wealth. Since the middle of the nineteenth century we
have seen the rise of the gospel of work, the gospel of
wealth, the gospel of success. By 1901 Episcopal Bishop
William Lawrence could say, "Godliness is in league with
riches."[28] And with the idea that the godly are rich and the
rich are godly the idea of a covenant based on love was just
about gone.

My original article on civil religion was written in 1965
and published in 1967 in an issue of *Daedalus* on "Religion
in America." Looking back now it seems that the article
and the widespread response it evoked reflected some kind
of break in the line of American identity. Civil religion
came to consciousness just when it was ceasing to exist, or
when its existence had become questionable. Nor was it
only civil religion that was affected by the upheaval of the
sixties. Sydney Ahlstrom in his *Religious History of the
American People* speaks of the end of the "Puritan Era,"[29]
by which I think he means the Protestant hegemony of
American culture. But indeed all religious traditions in
America were called in question in that decade and are still
in doubt. The legitimacy and authority of all our institu-

28. William Lawrence, in Ralph Gabriel, *The Course of American Demo-cratic Thought* (New York: The Ronald Press, 1956), p. 158.
29. Sidney E. Ahlstrom, *A Religious History of the American People* (New Haven: Yale University Press, 1972), chap. 63.

tions, political, economic, educational, even familial, as well as religious, has never been shakier. We are, then, not only in an economic depression but in a political and religious one as well. This profound loss of confidence in our institutions and our traditional identities is even more serious than the economic troubles that seem to plague us chronically in recent years.

It is a situation of hope as well as danger. The coming-apart of unholy alliances, such as that between utilitarianism and biblical religion, could lead to some new imaginative visions, some alternatives to the ever-increasing dominance of governmental and corporate bureaucracy into which we have fallen. Only the biblical religions, I venture to think, can provide the energy and vision for a new turn in American history, perhaps a new understanding of covenant, which may be necessary not only to save ourselves but to keep us from destroying the rest of the world. Such a revitalization of biblical religion in America would find, I believe, an ally rather than an enemy in the highest aspect of the civil tradition.

Alas, we have no Jefferson or Lincoln today to educate us and rededicate us to our Revolutionary ideals. Or if we do, I have not yet discerned him or her. But that is no reason to despair. Our greatest leaders have always been exemplars and teachers, not dictators who did what the people could not do. If there are no great teachers, we must teach ourselves.

But if we let our heritage slip from our hands, if we do not understand what we are, then Lincoln's great words about us, words we find it hard to understand in these closing years of the twentieth century—that we are "the last best hope of earth"—will in the end be nothing but a mockery, a sarcastic epithet for a fallen republic.

CONTRIBUTORS

Jerald C. Brauer, the editor, is Naomi Shen-
stone Donnelley Professor of the History of
Christianity at the Divinity School, The Univer-
sity of Chicago. Sidney E. Mead is Professor
Emeritus in the Department of History and the
School of Religion at the University of Iowa,
Iowa City, and Robert Bellah is Ford Professor
of Sociology and Comparative Studies at the Uni-
versity of California at Berkeley as well as Vice-
Chairman for the Center of Japanese and Korean
Studies there.